How to be a Medium

How to be a Medium

W.H. Evans

Commonwealth Book Company

ISBN: 978-1-948986-56-4

CONTENTS

PART I

The Development and Practice of Mediumship

PAGE

Part One

THE DEVELOPMENT AND PRACTICE OF MEDIUMSHIP

CHAPTER I

INTRODUCTION

What are Psychic Phenomena ?—Description of the Facts—Mental Phenomena—What the Facts Mean.

What are Psychic Phenomena ?

Psychic phenomena fall into two groups termed physical and mental, or objective and subjective. Physical phenomena are those which affect the senses of the observer—they can be seen and felt ; the mental are those apprehended by the mind.

Physical phenomena comprise raps, movements of objects with or without contact, playing of musical instruments, handling fire with impunity, passage of matter through matter, apports, direct voice, writing and painting, materialization of spirit-forms, hands, faces, etc., exudation of ectoplasm, photographing spirits, and luminescent effects.

Mental phenomena comprise automatic and inspirational writing and drawing, impersonations and transfigurations, clairvoyance, clairaudience, prevision, and psychometry.

Physical and mental phenomena are usually associated, as for instance in automatic writing and entrancement of mediums with certain forms of physical effects.

Description of the Facts

Raps.—This form of psychic phenomena was first used by the spirit people to open up communication with us, and has aptly been termed "God's telegraph". The Rochester Knockings have passed into history and are now regarded as genuine, though theories of their origin vary. These raps often occur spontaneously and under varying conditions. Sir William Crookes wrote in his *Researches into the Phenomena of Modern Spiritualism*:

> With mediums, generally, it is necessary to sit for a formal séance before anything is heard; but in the case of Miss Fox it seems only necessary for her to place her hand on any substance for loud thuds to be heard in it, like a triple pulsation, sometimes loud enough to be heard several rooms off. In this manner I have heard them in a living tree—on a sheet of glass—on a stretched iron wire—on a stretched membrane—on the roof of a cab—and on the floor of a theatre. Moreover, actual contact is not always necessary; I have heard these sounds proceeding from the floor, walls, etc., when the medium's hands and feet were held—when she was standing on a chair—when she was suspended in a swing from the ceiling—when she was enclosed in a wire cage—and when she had fallen fainting on a sofa. I have heard them on a glass harmonicon—I have felt them on my own shoulder and under my own hands. I have heard them on a sheet of paper, held between the fingers, by a piece of thread passed through one corner.
>
> With a full knowledge of the theories which have been started, chiefly in America, to explain these sounds, I have tested them in every way that I could devise, until there has been no escape from the conviction that they were objective occurrences not produced by trickery or mechanical means.

This testimony is so clear that no one with any knowledge of the work done by Sir William Crookes in the world of science can doubt the reality of these raps. Moreover his testimony is borne out by that of thousands of people who have heard these percussive sounds.

Movements of Objects.—The commonest form of this phenomenon is that of table-tilting. It is so well known and is so easily tested that many people having no knowledge of Spiritualism accept the fact, merely regarding it as a kind of parlour game. Movements without contact are more rare, but very convincing, and generally more evidential. Levitation is a well attested phenomenon, and the testimony of Lord Lindsay, Lord Adare, and Capt. Charles Wynne, concerning the occasion when D. D. Home was wafted out of one window and in through another at Ashley House, off Victoria Street, London, is so weighty that few can doubt it.

Playing of Musical Instruments.—This also is a well attested fact, and I have heard a small auto-harp played, in a good light, without contact.

Handling of Fire.—The classic instance is recorded in the Book of Daniel. It is also recorded of D. D. Home that he took a live coal from the fire and placed it on the head of Mr. S. C. Hall, then editor of the *Art Journal*, and drew his white hair up around it so that the glowing coal could be seen through the strands of white hair. No harm was done to a single hair! A personal friend of mine, Mr. C. Adams of Plymouth, often handled fire with impunity.

Passage of Matter through Matter.—The bringing of objects into closed rooms, the doors of which are locked, is not an uncommon phenomenon. I have experienced this on several occasions. It sometimes happens at psychical séances that the medium's coat is taken off, even when he is securely bound to his chair, the rope being undisturbed.

Apports.—The bringing of objects from a distance: clay tablets, coins, live birds, fish, pieces of coral, and numerous other things. One of the most astounding on record is the flight of Mrs. Guppy across London from Highbury to Bloomsbury. The parallel to this may be read in Acts viii, 39, where it says: "The Spirit of the Lord caught away Philip from the desert near Gaza and took him to Azotus", a distance of forty miles. The marvel in Mrs. Guppy's case is not only the flight but her entry into a closed room!

Direct Voice, Writing, and Painting.—The speaking of spirits direct to those assembled at séances, either through a trumpet or without, is well known. Many cases are on record, and valuable evidence of spirit-communication has been obtained in this way.

Writing and painting accomplished direct, without any visible means. Crookes records an instance of direct writing, and Vice-Admiral Usborne Moore records his experiences with various mediums who produced paintings on canvas by psychic means, in full daylight.

Materializations.—This varies from the exudation of ectoplasm to the formation of hands, faces, and full-forms. Sir William Crookes, who tested this phenomenon, tells us that he took many photographs of the materialized form of Katie King. Many other prominent scientists since his day have testified to the reality of materializations, notably Richet, Schrenck, Notzing, and Geley.

Luminescent Effects.—These are lights of varying size and brilliancy. I have seen them on many occasions, and at one séance, held without any preliminary notice, had the pleasure of having them float into my hand.

Psychic Photography.—This is still a much disputed phenomenon, but the number of evidential photographs of deceased persons indicates that it is real. One feels that in this aspect of mediumship the phenomena are too haphazard; one may sit and everything be genuine and above-board, yet get an extra which no one can recognize. Is it not possible for the medium's guides so to act that only extras of relatives and friends who can readily be recognized may appear on the plate? It should be possible. Skotographs are extras appearing on plates which have not been exposed. Quite a number of supernormal pictures have been obtained in this way.

Mental Phenomena

Automatic Writing and Drawing.—So called because the medium writes or draws with no conscious volition. Sometimes he is entranced; at other times the sensitive may engage in reading or conversation, although writing. Automatic drawings are mainly symbolic in character, though the work done through David Duguid was chiefly the painting of landscapes. The symbolism of automatic drawing is rarely understood and seems to have little real value. Of automatic scripts, the writings of the Rev. Stainton Moses and Miss Geraldine Cummins are classical examples.

Inspirational Writing and Speaking.—This differs from the former in that the matter flows through the mind of the medium. As "all inspiration is governed by the channel through which it flows", it follows that the more cultured the medium the clearer the inspiration is likely to be. Much that today is published as inspirational script would benefit by careful editing. Unfortunately, a false reverence for the written word is responsible for the publication of matter whose destiny should be the waste-paper basket.

Trance.—This varies in depth; it should not be considered as synonymous with unconsciousness. Many people think that every medium who closes his eyes is unconscious of his surroundings; as a matter of fact I consider that unconsciousness is comparatively rare. The commonest form of trance is comparable to the dream state. The trance is necessary for certain forms of phenomena such as materializations, transfigurations, and for the giving of messages and addresses.

Clairvoyance.—This is literally clear-seeing: the power to see and describe spirits, symbols, scenes, etc. It varies in degree and manifestation, some getting vivid impressions (clairsentience) which they visualize, while some see visions as objective realities. Distance is no barrier, and clairvoyants occasionally are able to describe scenes happening many miles away.

Clairaudience.—The hearing of various sounds and voices; a purely subjective state, which if not regularized can be very annoying. Sometimes it can be induced by listening to the sounds in a seashell, but it is not wise to force matters.

Psychometry.—The reading of character from objects which have been in close contact with people, or from letters, photos, etc.; the diagnosing of disease; the recovery of past history from the auras of articles;

literally the reading of the etheric records associated with things.

Prevision.—This faculty of foretelling future events is one which forms part of every religion, and the prophet, whether as a great preacher or the foreteller of future happenings, fills a large part in the history of religion. It is a form of clairvoyance.

What the Facts Mean

The variety and richness of the phenomena will now be apparent. It will be realized that to separate them, except for the purposes of study, is foolish. A review of the facts reveals, firstly, the existence of some hitherto unknown force by which the effects are produced, and, secondly, that the phenomena are accompanied by some intelligence which is able to direct the force so that with one medium it will manifest physically, and with another mentally. "There are diversities of gifts but the same spirit." Let us take one of the simplest forms of psychic phenomena and consider it.

If we sit for table-tilting, we shall speedily discover that the table will move without our being able to account for the movement. Who or what moves it? We may presume that some force is operative, but our assumption accounts only for the movements, not for the intelligence. Presumably the force emanates from the medium and sitters. Sir William Crookes called it "psychic force". To many investigators it is not a blind, or even unconscious, power, for it moulds the ectoplasm, or moves objects, and is considered to have some bearing upon biological phenomena. Thus the fact that the ectoplasm is moulded into hands and faces, or fully formed human bodies, is regarded as offering evidence that it is a substance through which some form of psychic energy acts according to some directive idea, this being the same as the particular form of life that may be manifest. It is considered that the psycho-dynamism of the medium moulds the ectoplasm into feet, hands, faces, etc. From this it will be seen that associated with the simple tilting of a table there is an intelligence which must be accounted for. When considering the objective phenomena, scientific caution is justified in narrowing the field, but by persisting in so doing caution is apt to degenerate into dogmatism.

To get a fuller understanding of the phenomenon of materialization, we will consider the evidence of Sir William Crookes. He writes:

> I pass on to a séance held last night at Hackney. Katie [the materialized form] appeared to greater perfection, and for nearly two hours she walked about the room, conversing familiarly with those present. On several occasions she took my arm when walking, and the impression conveyed to my mind that it was a living woman by my side, instead of a visitor from the other world, was so strong that the temptation to repeat a recent celebrated experiment became almost irresistible. Feeling, however, that if I had not a spirit, I had at all events a *lady* close to me, I asked her permission to clasp her in my arms, so as to be able to verify the interesting observations which a bold experimentalist has recently somewhat verbosely recorded.
>
> Permission was graciously given, and I accordingly did—well—as any gentleman would do under the circumstances. Mr. Volckman will be pleased to know that I can corroborate his statement that the "ghost" (not "struggling", however) was as material a being as Miss Cook herself. But the sequel shows how wrong it is for an experimentalist, however accurate his observations may be,

to venture to draw an important conclusion from an insufficient amount of evidence.

Katie now said she thought she should be able this time to show herself and Miss Cook together. I was to turn the gas out, and then come with my phosphorus lamp into the room now used as a cabinet. This I did, having previously asked a friend who was skilful at shorthand to take down any statement I might make when in the cabinet, knowing the importance attaching to first impressions, and not wishing to leave more to memory than necessary. His notes are now before me.

I went cautiously into the room, it being dark, and felt about for Miss Cook. I found her crouching on the floor. Kneeling down, I let air enter the lamp, and by its light I saw the young lady dressed in black velvet, as she had been in the early part of the evening, and to appearance perfectly senseless; she did not move when I took her hand and held the light quite close to her face, but continued quietly breathing. Raising the lamp, I looked around and saw Katie standing close behind Miss Cook. She was robed in flowing white drapery as we had seen her previously during the séance. Holding one of Miss Cook's hands in mine, and still kneeling, I passed the lamp up and down so as to illuminate Katie's whole figure, and satisfy myself thoroughly that I was really looking at the veritable Katie whom I had clasped in my arms a few minutes before, and not the phantasm of a disordered brain. She did not speak, but moved her head and smiled in recognition.

Three separate times did I carefully examine Miss Cook crouching before me, to be sure that the hand I held was that of a living woman, and three separate times did I turn my lamp to Katie to examine her with steadfast scrutiny, until I had no doubt whatever of her objective reality. At last Miss Cook moved slightly, and Katie instantly motioned me to go away. I went to another part of the cabinet, and then ceased to see Katie, but did not leave the room till Miss Cook woke up, and two of the visitors came in with a light.

Here we have the calm, sober statement of an eminent scientist. Such experiences might be multiplied, but one is sufficient for our purpose. What is the meaning of such a fact? Are we to consider that the sub-conscious mind of Miss Cook was able, when the normal consciousness was in abeyance, to build up from the ectoplasmic emanations of her body a complete human form entirely unlike herself, and with an altogether different personality? To say the least, such an assumption makes an even greater demand upon our credulity than an acceptance of what the fact seems to imply—namely, that Katie was a separate personality who had a knowledge of the technique necessary for producing such a phenomenon. This knowledge must have been extensive, as such a manifestation implies a comprehensive understanding of physics, biology, physiology, and psychology, as all these sciences are involved in such a manifestation.

The common-sense person will put theorizing on one side and declare that Katie was what she claimed to be, and certainly if we met a materialized form in the street, without knowing it to be such, we should not regard it as the manifestation of someone's sub-conscious mind, but a real person.

When we turn to the consideration of the subjective phenomena, we find the evidence for an independent intelligence increases. Sunday after Sunday on Spiritualist platforms clairvoyant descriptions are given, and also trance addresses. Often evidences of distinctive personalities are conveyed to people in the audience. One may shout "telepathy", but you cannot explain one mystery by introducing another. To say that the mediums get into contact with the minds of those to whom they are giving messages does not give light, for immediately we wish to know the mode of procedure. Telepathy is as great a mystery to us as that of a spirit conveying

to us his message. To refuse to accept a fact because we do not know the "how" of it is not only unscientific but foolish.

What does the fact of clairvoyance mean? An extension of faculty? Very well—for what purpose? Why describe spirits if they are not there? Why should our sub-conscious minds combine to deceive us?—for there must be collaboration between our sub-consciousness and that of the medium. If we accept the facts at their face value, it may not lessen the mystery, but it does help to a clearer understanding of our being.

The vast amount of automatic and inspirational writing which pours from the press affords much evidence of the action of minds other than that of those mediums through whom the writing is given. Cross-correspondences and book-tests give further evidence of spirit action. Photographs of deceased persons, sometimes of those of whom no photograph is in existence, also weight down the scale on the "side of the angels".

From all the varieties of psychic phenomena there emerges one claim made with consistent emphasis: it is that they are produced by the spirits of departed human beings. One does not rule out supplementary theories, for it would be foolish to affirm that any and every phenomenon is the outcome of direct spirit agency. We must remember that we also possess whatever power is used by spirits to produce any psychic effect. There are occasions when it acts automatically—that is, without conscious effort either on our part or that of spirits. In these cases we find an absence of intelligent direction, and a lack of response when any questions are addressed to it. One may compare this power to electricity, which in a thunder-storm acts without intelligent direction, but which in a power house is directed into channels where it can be of service. The consensus of evidence for the action of spirits operating with a definite purpose in the phenomena which occur in the séance-room is overwhelming.

The existence of some hitherto unknown force with which the spirits of the dead are associated is a fact of great importance. From it we deduce that the primary meaning of the facts is to prove the existence of a world more ethereal than this, that we pass into it at death with our individualities unimpaired, and will, under appropriate conditions and should we so desire, be able to commune with those whom we have left behind.

CHAPTER II

MEDIUMS AND MEDIUMSHIP

The Necessity for a Medium—What is a Medium ?—Distinction Between Medium and Psychic—Psychic Faculty in Sleep—Trance Consciousness.

The Necessity for a Medium

One of the difficulties in the minds of many would-be investigators of Spiritualism is expressed in the phrase: "If my friends in the other life wished to communicate, they would come to me ; they would not go to a medium. Why should it be necessary for me to go to a medium to converse with them ?" The thought in the mind of the objector is that if communion is possible, we must have in our nature those psychic qualities by which our spirit-friends can communicate with us. Thinking thus, it is imagined that such communion is an easy and simple matter, but experience shows that communion between us and the spirit-world is neither easy nor simple. Whenever opportunities and conditions are appropriate, communion is possible. For everything in life a medium of some kind is required.

The inquirer then often shifts his ground and asks: "But if so-and-so can see spirits, why can't I ?" Well, probably he can—if he has the power and will to strive to develop it. But that is not sufficient. St. Paul says: "There are diversities of gifts", a statement which applies to all human powers. To one is given the gift of words, to another that of song, to another the gift of painting or sculpture, etc. We do not ask, because so-and-so is a great singer, "Why cannot I sing?" for we know that unless we have the gift we cannot become singers. Spiritual gifts, like natural gifts, are diverse; to one is given the power of seeing, to another of hearing the spirits, or the power of healing the sick, or one of the many psychic gifts with which we are acquainted.

Next the inquirer assumes that his spirit friends do not come to him. This is entirely wrong—they do; but finding either that he is psychically obtuse, or has, through prejudice, shut the door, they are unable to make any impression upon him. They can only wait some appropriate season when he chances to be in the company of someone who can see or sense spirit people. Then he is told: "I see *by you* a spirit friend"—the medium merely acts as the messenger delivering a telegram, and conveys as clearly as he can the message he is entrusted to deliver. Often, after he has received such a message, the seeker realizes the possibilities, and turns his attention to psychic matters. This movement of his mind breaks down the prejudice and makes it possible for his own psychic faculty to function. He becomes his own medium! He then realizes that to complain about the necessity for a medium is as reasonable as to grumble that he cannot write like Shakespeare, or compose like Beethoven. He realizes that mediumship comes within the orbit of law, as does everything else in the universe.

WHAT IS A MEDIUM?

From the foregoing we have seen that there are conditions associated with every phenomenon: cause, means, end—the means is the medium. That a human being is the medium for the production of psychic phenomena is due to the nature of the facts, which are biological and mental rather than physical.

A medium is a person whose organism supplies the necessary force for the production of the various psychical phenomena already described, or whose organism is used for the various mental effects mentioned.

Psychic phenomena reveal that man lives in more worlds than one. Broadly speaking, we are only conscious of the material aspects of the universe, but there are also numerous vibrations from the psychic and spiritual realms. These affect our sub-consciousness, sometimes emerging in our waking life as visionary or auditory experiences. The development of mediumship makes us, in some degree, aware of those worlds which lie beyond the fringe of our ordinary sense-perception.

The facts of mediumship imply that we have more than one body—the physical body which relates us to, and brings us into contact with, the material world; and the psychic body which relates us to the inner worlds of life. As our consciousness is focused in our material brains we are not usually cognisant of the higher worlds, and the more the mind is engaged with material things, the more remote does the psychic and spiritual appear. Yet the material world is interpenetrated by the psychic and spiritual; man is a spiritual being.

The qualities and powers of the psychic body are latent in most of us. When they become active we have the phenomena of mediumship. This may not increase the spirituality of the sensitive; not until the higher consciousness is awakened do these powers bring one into contact with the heavenly planes.

In responding to a higher influence there is usually, with whatever comes through, an admixture from the sub-conscious mind of the medium. One of the difficulties associated with mediumistic development is that of separating the sub-conscious impressions of the medium from the messages emanating from another mind. Here we need the full use of our critical faculties and must not be too eager to accept everything which comes through the mouth of a sensitive. Those in the higher life always urge us to exercise our own judgment upon whatever comes through. One of the great obstacles in the way of mediumistic development is that mediums are apt to be satisfied with too low a level.

Distinction Between Medium and Psychic

The psychic body is linked to the physical body by lines of magnetic force. There is a constant interchange of energy going on between them, and so long as this interchange is unimpeded, a state of health exists. The phenomenon of spirit-control associated with many forms of mediumship is brought about by a spirit manipulating the forces connecting the various bodies.

A psychic, who may also be a medium, is one who has gained some measure of control of the finer elements and can consciously exercise his powers. To some degree he seems independent of spirit help, though even with psychics spirits often manifest. Among those in the Spiritualist movement there is a certain looseness of expression which confuses mediums with psychics. The psychic is more positive than the medium, who relies entirely upon the efforts of his guides to convey their messages. Many criticize the passivity demanded for the development of mediumship as likely to weaken character. The criticism is entirely misplaced, as the development of mediumship generally results in an all-round strengthening of the individual. As far as strength is concerned the medium is as strong as the psychic, and is often able to go very much farther than the psychic and touch deeper realms of life. Mediumship itself leads to the mastery of the psychic forces of the body, and I consider it a far safer road than that so often advocated by those who proclaim the blessings of Yoga.

Psychic Faculty in Sleep

"We are such stuff as dreams are made of", said Prospero. May we borrow his magic wand and see if we can discover a little of the magic world of dream into which we enter at night? Emerson declared that

> we all have one key to the miracle of the poet, and the dunce has experiences which may explain Shakespeare to him—one key—namely, dreams. In dreams we are true poets; we create the persons of the drama; we give them appropriate figures, faces, costume; they are perfect in their organs, attitude, manners. Moreover, they speak after their own characters, not ours; they speak *to* us, and we listen with surprise to what they say.

Indeed, I doubt if the best poet has yet written any five-act play that can compare in thoroughness of invention with this unwritten play in fifty acts, composed by the dullest snorer on the floor of the watch-house.

We all dream at times, and we usually dismiss our nightly experiences as mere stuff resulting from disturbed digestion. That this should give rise to these images rarely excites our wonder, and we regard our dreams as meaningless and dismiss them as of no consequence.

One of the most significant facts of our dream life is that we maintain our identity. No matter what absurdities we perform, or how ridiculous may be the situations in which we find ourselves, we are essentially ourselves. This fact does not seem to have been so carefully considered as it deserves. Always the dream is considered unreal, but in the midst of this unreal world we live, move, and act as logically—for even the absurdities of our dream state have a logical basis—as we do in our waking life. Another fact is that two at least of our senses seem active. We see and hear in dreams. With what eyes do we see and with what ears do we hear? Our physical eyes are closed and our hearing is inactive.

The explanation of dreams as being due to some physical excitation does not seem to cover the facts. Our sense of individuality is as vivid as in our waking state, and our consciousness of the body we use equally so. It is not a case of imagining ourselves in certain situations, as we may do in reverie; we are not conscious of imagining: *we are only conscious that we exist.* There are some dream experiences which seem to indicate that our psychic faculty is active. It is in prophetic dreams that this seems evident. In such dream states there is neither past nor future; in dreams the future happening is seen as present. It is in our waking life that the factor of time manifests.

Dr. Abercrombie records a case of a young man who dreamed of climbing Mount Etna and, on reaching the summit, going down into the crater. Ten years elapsed before he performed what he had dreamed.

Dame Edith Lyttleton told in her broadcast talk on "Foreknowledge" the case of a medical student who, on June 5, 1859, dreamed that on June 9, 1864, five years later, a terrible calamity would overtake him. He could not remember details, but the date was forcibly impressed on his memory. He went to the surgery and told the assistant surgeon that some disaster would come upon him in five years. Then he wrote the date, June 9, 1864, on the underpart of the mantel-piece, and signed his initials. Later he left the profession, went into business, and forgot all about his dream. On June 9, 1863, he married. On June 8, 1864, his wife was desperately ill, and when the doctor came downstairs and said, "There is no hope for your wife", the recollection of the dream came like a flash of lightning to his mind. His wife died the next day, June 9, 1864.

Such experiences indicate that we possess powers which transcend our normal consciousness and seem to belong to another order of existence.

One of the most remarkable cases of psychic faculty in sleep is that of the blind woman spoken of by Harriet Martineau. This woman had been blind from birth, yet she had vivid dreams, her descriptions of which indicated that she was, in sleep, clairvoyant, for she spoke of the people she saw, the clothes they wore, their colours, as well as scenes. How explain this? She had never had visual experiences—how then did she see? What was the organ of perception? It reminds us of St. Paul's words: "There is a spiritual body". May we not accept this as a statement of fact? If we do we shall understand the reason for the blind woman seeing; she functioned in her spiritual body. As a theory it works, even better than some with more long-sounding names.

Trance Consciousness

The word trance is used very loosely, mainly because people think that it means a state of complete unconsciousness.

Actually, it is analogous to the dream state, with this difference, that the trance may be very light, the sensitive being more or less aware of what is going on around him. The trance condition varies from the impulse to close the eyes to shut out external impressions, through varying stages, to complete unconsciousness.

Spiritualists speak of trance as a condition induced in a medium by some spirit. Certainly those who become trance mediums have rarely experienced it before developing. The condition is similar to that induced by hypnotists, and we shall see presently that the means used by spirits to entrance a medium are similar to those used by hypnotists.

Mediums who are frequently used by spirit controls are not usually readily amenable to hypnosis. The controls exercise a watchful care of their mediums, and do not allow them to be influenced by others. They build up around their sensitives a protecting psychic wall which keeps out intruders and, unless the mediums' guides allow, no hypnotist can break through. Moreover, it protects the sensitive from any wanderers in the borderland so that they do not become the victims of obsession. It is a mistake to think that the development of mediumship renders one liable to obsession. It is, when rightly developed and used, the surest protection against it.

The continuous exercise of the psychic faculty tends to the formation and development of a mediumistic personality. That is, a part of the sensitive's consciousness is educated by the guides to act on their behalf when necessary. The emergence of this personality is dependent upon the action of the guides who make use of it to carry on their work. The activity of this personality seems to depend upon the degree of entrancement of the medium. It emerges in the lighter forms of trance and displays qualities pertaining to the medium's own self. Hence in some forms of spirit control we get a great deal of the medium and very little of the guide. Much depends upon conditions.

It will be seen that the trance state varies even with the same medium. We have not yet discovered why information can be clearly conveyed at one time when the medium is only one degree removed from normal consciousness, while at others information can only be given when the medium is completely unconscious.

Probably it depends upon the degree of rapport between medium and guide. We know that if we have two tuning-forks of the same pitch and one is struck, the other will respond. If the mind of the medium happens to be in a state in which it synchronizes with that of his guide, information can the more readily be conveyed.

The reason for deepening the trance is probably this need of bringing the sensitive's mind into harmony with that of the control. It is unwise to accept everything which comes through a sensitive under control. Spirits are human and sometimes make mistakes. The idea that death makes one omniscient is a mistaken one. We have to bring what we are told to the bar of our reason, and pass judgment upon it. On no account should we get into the habit of depending upon advice from those over the border. We are here to grow.

What happens when a medium is controlled? First—and here I speak from personal experience—there is a heightening of perception. The sense of hearing becomes abnormally acute; sounds become amplified to such a degree as to be almost hurtful. One can hear his audience breathe, while the ticking of a clock is like the blows of a hammer. Perhaps you have observed in a half-awake condition that any sudden sound seems very much louder than it actually is. The first state of trance is similar. It speedily gives way to a feeling of drowsiness; there is a sense of falling backwards, and then sleep (or trance) ensues. Thereafter, one knows nothing until one wakes up—or, as we say, the spirit leaves control. Perhaps the clearest description of how spirit control is effected is that given by Tien Sien Tie, the control of Mr. J. J. Morse. He says:

> The operation is mesmeric. It depends largely upon circumstances what method is employed. Usually, to begin with, a slight effort is directed to the heart, for the purpose of lowering the rate of circulation. This induces a primary lethargy, slight in itself, but sufficient. The action is then directed, sometimes to the solar plexus, for the purpose of affecting the nervous

system. By this process we reach the brain, usually the basilar portion first, which represents the physical side of the individual, thereby securing control, so to speak, of the circulation, the nervous system, and the vital forces. This leaves the front, or upper brain, in a state of more than usual activity. By the time the first half of the control, however, has been established, we are able to reach the sensorium by the action of the will upon the psychical forces, through the nervous system—of sensation this time. The sense of lethargy increases, the blood slightly recedes from the outer blood-vessels, and the phenomenon of sleep immediately ensues.

At this point the will is intensely excited, so that a domination is established over the entire body, brain, nervous and vital forces. A sense of falling backward is experienced and the physical consciousness departs. At this period there is a lull in the bodily actions, and the vital forces are now restimulated to a certain degree, the nervous activity re-excited, and the psychical forces are set into operation for the purpose of what I can only best describe as waking up the inside of the brain ; or, to put it perhaps more clearly, of stimulating the spiritual or subjective faculties of the man. Then follows a rather delicate operation of discharging a sufficient amount of vital energy through the base of the brain, the lower brain, so that it can be made to act without altering the lethargic condition of the heart. When this has been accomplished, the body becomes erect, and the various functions are at our service, the organ of speech can be manipulated, and the machine is in working order.

So far, so good. If, however, there has been any great disturbing circumstance, either painful or pleasurable, in the course of the day, the effects of which are still left on the brain and on the nerves, such disturbance has to be overcome. Sometimes this is accomplished by driving it on one side, as you might blow a cloud away ; sometimes it is held in check, and little by little worked into the subject of the discourse we are delivering—absorbed, so to speak, as the best way of getting rid of it. If there is a physical disturbance inside the organism, that has to be attended to also, held in check, reduced or what not, as the case may demand ; so you can readily understand, when all these points have to be considered, that the task of effecting control, and carrying it through to a successful issue, is neither slight nor unimportant.

In these matters I receive much valuable assistance from my friend the "Player". Then, by using all the faculties of the brain which are brought into sympathetic relationship to my will, I literally play upon the brain as the piano-player plays upon the keys, with the result that, instead of music as from an instrument you have speech as from a man.

It will be seen from this that the process of controlling a medium is similar to that used to hypnotize a subject.

It is interesting to note the manner in which the trance state varies, even while the spirit is controlling the sensitive. Sometimes there are alternations of consciousness which produce in the mind of the sensitive a state of confusion. For instance, the trance being induced, the sensitive lapses into unconsciousness, in which state he begins his address. Then there is a temporary recovery, and the sensitive finds himself uttering a stream of words which convey no meaning to him. This is followed by a lapse into the deeper state, with again, after a while, a return of consciousness. This pendulum-like swing of consciousness may persist all through the address, with the result that the sensitive, losing all track of any coherent argument, thinks that the control must be making a horrid mess of it.

The listener, of course, may be enjoying the discourse that is being given. The hiatus in the mind of the medium has no effect upon the delivery of the speech. Probably this alternation is due to some circumstance such as Tien mentions, which the control may have difficulty in keeping in check.

One other feature which has been noted is that often trance addresses are verbose, diffuse, and sometimes rambling. We have to remember that it is not like direct speech, and when we bear in mind that many mediums are uneducated and cannot in their normal state convey any information without much circumlocution, the task of the control will be seen to be no easy one. If you closely observe the utterances of trance mediums you will note three stages. The first may be described as getting under way. A few introductory remarks of a general character are given, followed by some really good matter. Then comes the withdrawal of the control, and at this stage there is frequently a repetition of what has already been said, with the result that what might have been a brilliant address is hopelessly spoiled. I may say that normal speakers may sometimes present the same features. The untrained speaker, not knowing when he has finished, may go on to spoil his effect by repetition.

It will be seen, then, that the dream state and the trance state have points in common, though the latter is usually more potent. The trance state sometimes evinces the same inability to come to grips with any matter, such as we experience in dreams. It seems that the development of trance mediumship is, in some degree, a development of the dream consciousness directed and controlled by a spirit for a definite purpose.

CHAPTER III

THE DEVELOPMENT OF MEDIUMSHIP

The Right Approach—The Religious View—What are Conditions ?—What May Happen—Mental States.

THE RIGHT APPROACH

WHEN people become interested in Spiritualism and find it is possible through the channel of mediumship to get into communication with their friends on the other side of death, they naturally desire to know whether they are mediums and, if so, how their powers may be developed. It is necessary to ask ourselves whether we seek the unfoldment of these powers from right motive. Many people are attracted by the novelty of the experience, and often through vanity wish to exercise what, to them, seem very mysterious powers. It is a pity there should be so many misconceptions about the matter, for mediumship is a sacred office, and no one should attempt to unlock their hidden powers unless they are prepared to use them on behalf of humanity. This does not mean that one may not become a professional medium ; to take money for the exercise of one's mediumistic powers is no more wrong than for a priest to do so, for "he that serves the altar must be kept by the altar".

We cannot too strongly deprecate the mystery with

which some people surround what is, after all, a power natural to the race. That it is more active in some than in others we have seen, but if anyone imagines that the development of mediumship puts them in possession of powers which will make them superior to their fellows, or enable them to dominate others by the weight of superior personality, as some catch-penny advertisements would have them believe, they had better leave the matter severely alone. There is an element of danger to all who seek to exploit these powers, and unless the motive is pure, the will firm, and self-control reasonably good, it is best to leave the development of psychic faculty alone.

One can feel sympathy with those who argue that no one should attempt to develop their psychic powers, but should await their natural manifestation ; but there must be pioneers to explore new territory and break new ground. Very little progress would be made if we all waited for our psychic powers to blossom. We can see what is feared by those who suggest such a course, but it is wise to overcome fear and not shrink from the unknown simply because it *is* unknown.

The right approach is to have quiet confidence in the unseen, and to have pure motives for seeking to get into touch with the next stage of existence.

The Religious View

Although many affirm that Spiritualism is not a religion, there is associated with its phenomena a definite religious atmosphere. The exercise of psychic faculty is generally accompanied by emotion, and the natural outlet for it is in some religious exercise. Many psychics, under stress of what is called the "power", feel a movement of the spirit which finds expression in prayer. This is usually more marked in the early stages of development; later, when the "power" is better controlled, the emotional stress is lessened. It is noticeable that when controls speak through mediums, they often do so in terms of religion. This is so even when the matter is of a scientific character, for spirits seem to have a keener God-awareness than the average human. For this reason a rational religious outlook can be of great help to anyone seeking development, but care should be taken that a maudlin sentimentality is not mistaken for religion. What passes for religion in some séances is simply an orgy of emotionalism, which exhausts and does not exhilarate the spirit, as does real religion. Personally, I find rich spiritual experience can be gained at seances; but it is wise to guard against emotional excess.

It is a good thing if the seeker has a sense of the sacredness of his powers, for that sense can be a fine protection and a great aid to deepening and enriching his whole being. After all, development of our psychic nature should make us not only better in the spiritual sense, but more efficient in every way. If it does not, there is something seriously wrong with our methods.

What are Conditions?

It is usual to begin séances with prayer, and I think it wise. Firstly, we have a recognition that we are spiritual beings with spiritual needs. Our minds are lifted to a higher plane. Secondly, our wish to develop our powers and meet the spirit people half-way is a help towards the end we desire. Thirdly, there is a unification of aspiration which tends to promote harmony, without which we shall find results poor, perhaps even entirely non-existent. This helps to bring about a fusion of forces, makes them circulate, so to speak.

Music, of the right kind, is also a fine help, but let it be *good* music. For this purpose a good gramophone with equally good records is better than a dozen people singing out of tune. The power of music is its effect upon the emotional nature. It helps to break down hardness and inhibitions of the mind, producing the mellowness of temper essential to those who wish to sense the inner realms of being.

One sometimes finds the atmosphere becoming dead, a condition of flatness, as if all energy had been earthed. Easy conversation, and even a joke causing the sitters to laugh heartily, may work wonders. The great essential is to keep the "power" flowing. A sensitive person can feel when the flow stops and will seek a means of promoting it by keeping the sitters in a bright state of mind.

In seeking development *it is not wise to sit alone.* There should always be someone present who has some knowledge of conditions, so as to be able to deal with any situation that may arise. Every circle should have an efficient conductor, who should be able to co-operate with the unseen, and be capable of sensing what the guides require. He should have sufficient knowledge of psychic matters to be able to place sitters in right relationship to one another. Circles should not be too long, nor held too often; for purposes of development twice a week is amply sufficient.

Not only should one go to a circle in the right frame of mind, but one should pay attention to bodily conditions. In a circle held many years ago at which extraordinary results were reported to have been obtained, the sitters adopted a non-flesh diet, abstained from alcohol and tobacco, and fasted for a time before the séance. This is excellent practice, and if a circle composed of the right sitters adopted similar practices, no doubt, provided that a mediumistic person was present, good results would accrue.

The minds of the sitters should be free from worry. Do not, if you can avoid it, take the cares of the world into the séance-room. Our friends in the higher life know our difficulties and, if they think it wise, will do their best to give us the advice and help we need. If we go loaded with care, we take with us a cloud that damps the atmosphere and makes it difficult for the spirit people to manifest their presence. Remember, the forces used are mental, and easily deflected. Obstinate scepticism and carping criticism can often prevent results. Keep an open mind, but not to the extent of becoming credulous and accepting everything coming through the lips of a medium as wisdom. Wisdom you will get, but sometimes undoubtedly it is mixed with folly. Use common sense, and learn to separate the wheat from the chaff.

There are two other conditions which should be observed. If possible, keep a room specially for séances. Next, have a fixed time for commencing your circle. This is important. If we make an appointment with anyone and they are late, we feel annoyed, especially if we are busy. Think of the communicating spirits as people like ourselves, who have many things to attend to. It is a mistake to think of spirit people as constantly by our side. One of the errors fostered by ignorant mediums is to tell people their friends are always with them. God help them; they must be bored to death! Think of being tied to a person all day and every day; why, even lovers grow tired of each other! No; be reasonable, think of spirits as like ourselves, and be as considerate in keeping your appointments with them as you are with your business friends. If you commence with a stated time, don't wait for late-comers; if they cannot be punctual, you must teach them the value of time—your time and that of your spirit friends.

Psychic development is not a haphazard undertaking; it is a serious matter and must be carried out in the right frame of mind and with proper regard to essential conditions. Time is, perhaps, one of the most important.

What May Happen

Having gathered together and made our advances and gone through the opening exercises, such as singing a hymn, or listening to some good music, and having offered prayer for guidance, our circle of from five to nine people must await events. There is no need to sit in solemn silence; easy conversation (on non-controversial lines) is a great help. Crossing the legs should be avoided. If anyone is mediumistic, they will feel the "power". Their respiration becomes deeper, the heart is affected, and sometimes a feeling of exaltation possesses them, in which the mind enters a condition analogous to the dream state. Thoughts may rise spontaneously in the mind of the sensitive, and they should be spoken; even if they do not seem to have any relevance at the moment, often they will be found to apply to some-one present. When a medium shows signs of "control", the other sitters should not become alarmed; they will certainly feel interested. The control should be questioned in a kindly manner. Sometimes it is, at first, difficult for the control to speak, but usually by signs replies will be given.

If there should be spasmodic movements of a somewhat violent character, an appeal to the "control" to be careful of the sensitive will usually be effective. Here let me point out that mediums should not be encouraged to indulge in these movements, or to make grimaces. Some think it is a sign of power, which, of course, it is; but it is only a sign, and not always a necessary one.

Some sensitives do not get beyond this stage, partly because it is often accompanied by a pseudo-mystical feeling which is mistaken for spiritual growth. In the beginning, these movements are, no doubt, due to some spirit endeavouring to take control of the medium. But if the sensitive does not try to co-operate with the control, and thinks because of the mental uplift felt that it is all that is needed, the control may pass from the spirit to the medium's subconscious mind. There are such things as mediumistic secondary personalities, and even with developed mediums such manifest at times and may be mistaken for the guide. This may not be fraud; the initial influence probably emanates from the control, who may, because he has to attend to other duties, hand over his work to the medium's secondary personality, who will speak in the name of the guide. With the would-be medium, if he does not go beyond these early stages, we may reasonably conclude that there is no influence or power outside himself. I have known some to remain at this stage for years.

Having appealed to the control to moderate his violence, we none the less sometimes find, before the defences are sure, some spirit breaks through. Overcome by the novelty of the situation, he apparently does not wish to leave the sensitive. There is no need to be alarmed. Keep a level head. Make an appeal to his good nature—he will usually respond. If he still refuses, de-magnetize the sensitive by making passes from the chest upwards over the head. It is sometimes wise to break the circle and let everyone except the conductor leave the room. This causes a withdrawal of power and weakens the hold of the control over the sensitive, who speedily becomes normal.

Now the sensitive may protect himself by making up his mind to be master in his own house. Our bodies are the dwelling-places of our souls, and we should be masters in them. Tell your spirit friends clearly and emphatically that you will not allow them to use your organism at any time they wish, but only when you are prepared for them to do so, and let that time be when you are in séance. Do not encourage control when away from the circle, and do not be misled by a false vanity into thinking that you are unique, or in any way a wonderful person with a marvellous work to do. There are many such people in the Spiritualist movement, who mistake the uttering of pious platitudes for divine wisdom. Be rational and maintain common sense. Make up your mind that you will not allow any spirit when controlling you to do anything that you would not do in your normal state, or that you would be ashamed of.

Also, do not get into the habit of blaming the controls for any erratic conduct on your part, or take refuge in saying: "I said that when under control and I am not responsible." *You are, because you lent yourself to it.* Adopt the rule of accepting responsibility for whatever may be said through your lips when in trance, and your friends will always respect your principle. Remember that control is not a matter of being dominated by a spirit, but of co-operation of sensitive with spirit-guide.

The fear of obsession which some have is partly the result of ignorance, and partly the result of sad experience. The best protection against any danger is knowledge and, in this matter, a rational development of one's psychic powers. Fear is likely to break down one's defences. In a properly conducted circle, provided those seeking development observe the necessary conditions, there need be no danger. It is wise to keep the vital forces at a high level, as no spirit can invade and hold possession of anyone who is in good sound health. I have mentioned how to act in case of a recalcitrant control, but danger from this source can be entirely eliminated if the sensitive determines, as I have suggested, to be master in his own house.

We will now consider some of the mental states associated with the development of mediumship.

Mental States

The more we know of the working of consciousness, the better we shall comprehend those more subtle powers associated with mediumistic development. Dealing with the psychic side of our being, Andrew Jackson Davis gives a classification of mental states which is exceedingly helpful. Starting with our ordinary condition, he speaks of the psychological, sympathetic, somnambulic, clairvoyant, and spiritual states. This classification must not be regarded as rigid; any of these conditions may coexist. They should be considered as the many forms in which consciousness expresses itself. For our convenience we will consider them separately.

The Ordinary State

This results from the impressions made upon our minds by our surroundings. It is not a static condition, being subject, as are all mental states, to change. Mental concepts and beliefs rule our lives; it is what we believe about things, not the things themselves, which is of importance. Humanity has believed many things which subsequent study has proven to be untrue. The human mind is very impressionable and readily receptive of suggestions, and under appropriate conditions men will believe almost anything. When we are children we take our mental tone from those in authority, and there are millions of people in the world who have never thought of questioning the ideas which they have been taught in their childhood. They have a horror of doubt, not knowing that rational doubt is the beginning of wisdom.

We are very fond of facts, but these are of little value unless they excite us to think about them. What does a fact represent? When we ask that question we enter the realm of constructive imagination. We begin to theorize, and no progress in science is possible unless we construct theories and hypotheses to help us to understand something of what facts mean. While the collecting of facts, or the getting of data, is the first step in knowledge, it is the *use* we make of our data that is of supreme importance.

Looked at thus, we see that our civilization is the symbol of what we collectively think. It is an expression of our inner life. Our laws, philosophies, sciences, religions are outgrowths of human consciousness which we have clothed in appropriate forms. The mistake we so often make is to regard the form as the real, when it is only the husk, or symbol of it. No form of society can be final; it is in a state of flux and changes as men change. The basis of our civilization is human consciousness expressed in our ordinary state.

The more we study psychic phenomena, the more convinced we become that in range and variety they present a very rich field for our investigation. We perceive that here too, facts are but symbols of inward realities, and as knowledge of them spreads, we shall see them grow in influence and power, changing the outlook of men and making them realize that material existence is not all-important.

The Psychological State

This state may be natural or induced. Those who are naturally in the psychological condition readily take on any impressions from their surroundings. It is not a happy state to be in, for, unless there is stability of character, the individual will be like a weather-vane. People who are unduly influenced by their environment are usually in this state. Such rarely make good mediums. They veer around to every point of the compass, and accept every doctrine which attracts their attention. On the other hand, he who unites strong will with acute sensitiveness will reveal powers of mind akin to genius. Nevertheless, he is apt to be erratic in his conduct, and often goes down in the struggle of life when least expected.

People in the psychological state sometimes become obsessed with certain ideas which render their minds temporarily positive to all other influences. Religious literature is full of examples of such people. In olden times men rushed away to the deserts and became saints and hermits. Under the domination of religious ideas they cut themselves adrift from social intercourse with their fellows. Because they believed that sin and death entered the world through Eve's transgression, they refused to look upon any woman, sometimes even their own mothers. Regarding their bodies as vile, they ceased to wash themselves. They mortified the flesh under the impression that it purified the soul. Small wonder their imaginations became disturbed, and they were subject to hallucinations! The air became alive with devils tempting them; the suppression of their natural powers produced mental disturbances, and they thought themselves tempted by beautiful women who upon their approach became grinning fiends.

This was the natural consequence of their surrender of reason and common sense to certain ideas. They were—to use an old term—psychologized by the fear of hell and the desire to escape eternal damnation, and no self-inflicted torture was thought too severe which helped them to this end. The inherent selfishness of their beliefs and methods were not realized. The will of God had been revealed and, caught in the whirl of their emotions, they were hurried from one extreme to another.

The influence of mind upon mind is often seen in crowds. People will sometimes be convulsed with laughter simply upon hearing others laugh. Under the sway of oratory, a crowd becomes as one being. Dominated by one idea, it will do the most horrid or heroic things, without understanding the reason. Caught in the contagion of excitement, the members of the crowd are whirled away, and when reason returns will wonder why they did what has been accomplished. Fright is another form of the psychological state, in which the mind surrenders to the dominant influence, so that we lose our reason and are like a ship which has lost compass and rudder.

One could multiply instances, but I can only give a brief outline sufficient for the purpose of illustrating these mental states.

The Sympathetic State

Between the mind and body there is a profound sympathy ; so closely interwoven are mind and body that some regard mind as a mere function of the brain. There is also the sympathy between mind and environment, and mind and mind. This sympathy is an essential condition for success in all mediumistic and psychic activity. Sympathy is the root from which springs a multitude of ideas, for our minds are influenced by many things. Attraction excites interest, and this often leads to our taking up various pursuits. Sympathy is warm, attractive; antipathy is cold, negative, and repellent. Each have their sphere of use, but both must be controlled by reason.

Around each person is an atmosphere which is called the aura, which the investigations of Dr. Kilner have placed on the map of science. The well-known radio-activity of matter suggests that even inanimate substances have their atmosphere. This is an important fact, indicating that the seen is merely a part of some greater whole, the substratum of which is invisible, but none the less real. Amongst men, the existence of the aura is felt even where it is not seen, for we all sense something of one another's general character, being either attracted or repelled by what we *feel*. Often we can give no reason for these feelings, which are the result of sympathetic or antipathetic vibrations affecting us through our auras. It is the basis of telepathic action. We see it manifest in those trivial and common experiences when we think of a person just before meeting them.

Psychometric power depends upon sympathetic contact with any person or article. It is a fact that we impress "something" of ourselves upon everything we touch, and the more we handle anything, the more does it absorb of our condition. The psychometrist, by sympathetic contact, is able to receive these influences and interpret them. It is one of the most marvellous powers of the human mind, and is at once the finest expression of that fundamental sympathy running throughout the universe.

The Transition State

The Spiritualist Movement affords many examples of this state. Many would-be mediums fall into the error of supposing that as soon as they are influenced by some exterior power, all is accomplished. Obsessed with the idea, which springs as much from wrong religious teaching as from vanity, that there is no further need for them to study and that their dear spirit friends will do all their thinking for them, they cease to read, or even to think; with the result that there is in their minds a constant iteration of one thought—there is no death and their loved ones return.

Spiritualist societies afford numerous examples of this type, and the lowering of the mental and spiritual tone of many churches is due to those in charge filling their platforms with people whose inefficiency is only equalled by their ignorance. These people imagine that if they remain ignorant it provides better proof of spirit activity. Really it does nothing of the kind; it merely affords proof of their incompetence, ignorance, and laziness. Obsessed with the thought that everything which comes through their lips, when in the psychic state, is high wisdom, they put their critical faculty to sleep. Unfortunately there are those of equal ignorance who puff such speakers up and speak of the wonderful addresses given by them. If you question these later as to what the addresses contained, they do not know; but the flow of language they declare was grand! Any idea that language is to express and *reveal* thought never enters their heads. So ready are some to accept as marvellous anything out of the ordinary, that they put their reason upon one side.

Here we see the confusion which may arise from those in the transition state. It cannot be too strongly emphasized that *on no condition must reason be suppressed.* Every manifestation of psychic power, every message claiming to be delivered under the power of inspiration, must be brought to the bar of reason. Some mediums would develop their powers to a far greater extent if they learned to make greater demands upon the unseen; to have a rational discontent with any state of partial development. The swing of the mind from the sublime to the ridiculous which occurs in the transition state would cease, and they would find their powers gradually increasing as they improved their abilities. Progress must be the keynote of the soul. We must ever strive for something higher; only thus can we get beyond the transition state.

The Somnambulic State

In this state we get evidence of the mind's independence of the bodily organism. Sleeping and waking are expressive of the law of periodicity. Diffused throughout Nature there is a vital principle which links suns and stars together, and from which springs the phenomena of the universe. When we lie down to sleep, we are as much in the care of this power as when we are awake. Few retain any recollection of their night-time experiences. Sometimes we bring back fragments, but the images arising from our partially awakened brains distort and jumble them into incoherency. Occasionally we have vivid dreams which impress us as being actual visions. These impress us with the importance of the spiritual life, and sometimes cause people to alter their lives. Perhaps when the spiritual development of the race has reached a higher standard there will be no period of unconsciousness; we shall at night step out of our bodies and function consciously upon another plane of being.

Somnambulism is an incipient manifestation of the spiritual faculties. It partakes in an inferior degree of clairvoyance. People have arisen in sleep and solved difficult problems which they could not do when awake, have done many things considered impossible; all of which indicates that the mind is superior to its instrument and can, when conditions are favourable, assert its superiority.

The Clairvoyant State

There is some degree of clairvoyance associated with every mental state, except the ordinary, but much that passes for it is not the pure condition which the term "clairvoyant state" implies.

The psychometrist, when interpreting impressions received from a letter or article, often sees mental pictures which rise spontaneously in his mind. Contact with an article releases the latent psychic energies, and the visualizing power of the seer acts automatically. The pictures conform to the influences which have, so to speak, brought them into being. These impressions are intensely vivid, so that the psychic mentally sees clearly and distinctly. Auditory impressions are often received, such as the names of people and places. Much that passes for clairvoyance at public meetings is mainly psychometric or telepathic in character, being a sensing by the medium of the conditions of those addressed.

There is also a mental clairvoyance, in which the mind receives sudden illuminations. Many mental workers experience this at times. The mind glows with light, which reveals new angles and facets of truth. In all creative work this phase of clairvoyance manifests. It has passed into the currency of everyday speech. We say, "I see", when we grasp some idea. It has a deeper significance than we usually assign to it ; it is indicative of a light which pervades the whole world, but which, in the words of the "Old Book", we cannot see because our "eyes are holden". We do not objectively see the world of ideas, conceptions, and thoughts in which we live and move.

When the clairvoyant faculty is active, the lower part of the forehead is illumined, and the seer looks through it as through a window ; hence, the closing of the eyes is a help to clear-seeing. Some say that the pituitary gland responds to a different rate of vibration and that it acts as an eye for this form of vision. That is a speculation ; we do not really know what centre of vision is affected when seeing clairvoyantly. We do know that in some cases of clairvoyance walls are as transparent as glass ; that things happening miles away are seen as if present before one; and sometimes glimpses of the spirit-world are caught. Wonderful as it is, it is not spiritual, though like every other faculty and power of our being it is affected by our conduct; but its presence and activity do not necessarily mean that the possessor is a saint. Not until we reach

The Spiritual State

can it be said that we enter the realm of mystical vision and understanding. This state embraces all the preceding conditions; it is the rounding-out and harmonizing of all the faculties of the mind, in which every function ministers to the whole man. An enlightened medium, who sees the principles underlying psychic phenomena, gradually awakens to the fact that within his soul is the power of divine illumination. He discerns that the exercise of any power must not be from motives of self-interest, but from the desire to be of service. It is this note of service which is the distinguishing sign of the spiritual state. The exalted mind no longer thinks of self, but only how it may be of help to others. Prayer becomes practical meditation, and not a selfish petition for personal comforts.

One may be in the spiritual state without being aware of the operation of any particular psychic faculty. There will be an all-embracing intuitive perception of truths and principles, which is higher than clairvoyance. It is seership, a state in which the soul reaches out and endeavours to explore the universe. A condition of mind which notes a fact only as a symbol of things spiritual. The seer lives in a world of his own; he obeys a higher law; and often when men are wrangling about questions of death, immortality, God, and such high matters, he can truly say he knows—and he who knows never argues. He may reason with another, but if that one is merely disputatious, desirous of showing off his intellectual alertness, he closes up, leaving his self-opinionated friend to discover for himself that which the enlightened one realizes he cannot reveal.

Another sign of this state is the individual's humble dignity; great souls go through life without making any fuss. They radiate an influence of goodwill, of quiet power; and sometimes, because of this, evoke antagonism from those who do not understand. One of the good and wise rules of life is to *watch your reactions*. Your response to the varying influences you contact will be an unfailing guide to your spiritual status. The reason why spiritually minded people sometimes evoke antagonism is that their presence makes those of lesser development feel uncomfortable. They realize their own inferiority, and resent it. Ponder on the antagonism Jesus evoked in the Scribes and Pharisees. Where there is enlightened vision, it darts beneath the crust of formula and creed and, extolling the spirit above the letter, arouses the opposition of the formalist. In every age there have been men of vision whom the bulk of mankind have condemned and sometimes put to shameful death.

The aim of all psychic unfoldment should be towards this high and exalted condition; but it must clearly be understood that the spiritual state is an eminently practical condition of mind. It is not to be reached by pious aspiration alone, nor when reached, to be passed in uttering pious platitudes. No! If the aspirant gets the vision to see clearly, he must work. *Increased vision brings increased responsibility.* We must enlarge our conception of the word spiritual. Spirit is the effective energy by which men do things. Inspiration does not belong to the priest alone, it is for the race; and wherever men aspire, comes the corresponding inspiration. The scientist in his laboratory can be inspired equally with the priest. Upon all is poured the quickening powers of the Spirit which, if we are open to receive them, will give a wider view and a deeper knowledge.

CHAPTER IV

THE DEVELOPMENT OF MEDIUMSHIP—*continued*

Table-tilting—Planchette and Ouija—Automatic Writing—Inspirational Writing—Clairvoyance—Clairaudience—Psychometry—Healing.

HAVING dealt in a general way with some aspects of mediumship and given an outline of the mental states associated with it, I now pass on to give more detailed directions for its development. I will begin with the simplest form of phenomena.

TABLE-TILTING

It need not be stressed that this so-called common form of physical phenomenon depends for its operation upon the possession of some "force" in the sitter or medium. Many people can get movements of tables who are not at all psychic in other directions, and often they are not aware of any definite feelings when they do use this power. Although good and evidential messages are at times obtained in this way, there is often confusion, while misleading messages are not unknown.

Some people can get table movements alone, others can only get them in co-operation with another sitter, but in either case the faculty should not be exercised too freely. The tendency amongst would-be mediums is to sit as frequently as possible, under the false idea that development is speeded up. What really happens is that there is a rapid dissipation of power with a consequent distortion in the messages, which make the phenomenon useless as a means of spirit communication.

As already stated, the approach should be right. The kind of table used does not seem to matter much, though some consider that a round table is preferable, as the force spreading through the magnetic field is itself circular in motion and can enfold the object more completely within its field of action. This is a matter of convenience. If one has not a round table, any shaped table will do ; I have even seen a chair used with complete success.

The sitters place their hands upon the surface of the table, taking care not to exert any pressure. Any movement is usually preceded by a tremor, which will be distinctly felt passing through the table, and often accompanied by breezes over the hands. After a while the table will move, and this is taken to indicate that there is a "presence" desirous of giving some message. The sitters must adopt a code so that understanding may be established between them and the communicator. The usual code is three tilts to signify "yes", two "doubtful", and one "no". If the movements are vigorous the alphabet should be called and often the table will move at every letter, stopping at the one required. This method is slow and cumbersome, but by its means messages are spelled out, the value of which the sitters must judge. This phenomenon is an elementary form of the more complex physical phenomena.

Sometimes, instead of movements, raps are heard, a

more decided and reliable form of communication. The same code can be used. Generally the information conveyed is more decided, definite, and evidential than that conveyed through the table.

One of the bugbears of table-tilting is the silly, misleading messages which come through, the source of which may be the sub-consciousness of the sitters, or mischievous spirits. It is difficult to suggest any means which will give complete protection, but it may be noted that uncertain results are obtained when the sitters make a too frequent appeal to the unseen. It is quite within reason that the communications may cause some confusion, with the object of trying to make people realize that they must rely more upon their own judgment, instead of running to spirits for help and advice. It is not the function of the spirit people to do for us that which we can well do for ourselves. Wrong ideas of spirit guidance are responsible for many of the trivial misdirections given through table-tilting. Where there is continuous misdirection the origin is probably the sub-conscious mind of the sitters. The power to move any object by these means is latent, and it will sometimes function without intelligent direction. On occasion there emerges a personality which spoils all attempts to obtain messages in this way. When this happens, the sitters should abandon the practice and seek development in some reliable circle amongst people who can be trusted, and whose mediumship ensures adequate protection.

It is clear from my observation that there is a pseudo mediumship which sometimes deceives even those with some knowledge of the genuine thing. Where there is genuine mediumship—and that means something more than this capacity for automatism—there is rarely any confusion. Some people get raps without any apparent reason. When they ask if there is anyone wishing to give a message, there is no response, indicating that the raps are merely an automatic explosion of psychic force. Such happenings do not always indicate any special mediumistic ability. Often the very best physical mediums have never experienced manifestations before coming into touch with Spiritualism.

That one does at times contact mischievous spirits is true, but the brand of humour is usually of a low type in which there is sometimes an element of cruelty. Such spirits may belong to what is called the elemental kingdom, which is said to be unmoral. We must not accept any message as finally authoritative; we have to use our reason. The individual who rushes to a table or a medium on any and every occasion to get a message is asking for trouble, and at the same time creating a mental and moral flabbiness he will have to overcome in the future. It is strength of character that is needed, therefore use any means of psychic development in a wise and commonsense manner.

Religiously inclined people make the sign of the cross over the table as a means of protection. This is not always effective. There is related a story of a bishop who tried to exorcize a spirit at a séance. The table continued to move, and in answer to a question spelled out: "I can't abide a bishop." After all, our protection lies in ourselves—that is, in our moral integrity—and not in any sign. The power of any word or sign is not in the sign or word itself, but in the faith and power of him who uses them. Nevertheless, an appeal to the higher powers is never disregarded, and mischievous spirits are frequently removed by those in the higher spheres.

It is sometimes argued that movements of the table are due to unconscious muscular action. This is possible, but it can easily be tested. A piece of paper under the hands will soon show whether one is exerting any unconscious pressure. If one does, the paper slides over the table, revealing that the movements are due to the pressure of the sitter.

With a powerful medium it is possible to get movements without contact. It is to be noted that when such occur the messages are usually veridical. Lack of physical contact seems to cut out any element of confusion, and the communicating intelligence is able to get its message through without the distortions so often experienced when the sitters are in direct physical contact with the object moved. Movement without contact is in itself evidence of a force acting independently of the minds of those present.

It is often objected that the messages obtained through table-tilting emanate from the minds of the sitters. That, the sitters must judge for themselves. Many evidential messages have been received which show clearly that they emanated from minds other than the sitters'.

Should the one sitting for table-tilting be decidedly physical in his mediumship, there will manifest clear evidence of his power. He may fall into trance. If this happens, there should be no alarm ; a quiet confidence should be maintained by other sitters present. I have already indicated what should be done in such a case. Here I need only state that there will be more abundant power manifested in the trance condition, with a corresponding development of the mediumship which will carry it to the more complex forms of physical phenomena. In these matters we can only seek intelligent co-operation with those at the other end of the line. When we do, we are met with a response that repays us for any little sacrifice we may have to make to stabilize the faculty.

Planchette and Ouija

Allied to the movement of objects is the use of those well-known forms, such as planchette, ouija (*we-ja*) board, and other varieties of simple apparatus. One can construct his own ouija board by marking the letters of the alphabet on a table with the words : Yes, No, Doubtful, and the necessary numerals. An upturned tumbler will do as a pointer. The fingers are placed on the tumbler which then moves to the various letters, spelling out words and answering questions. It is a quicker form of communication than table-tilting, but in this, likewise, there must be care and common sense, for the same elements which distort messages in table-tilting may manifest in this. The advice already given should be observed here.

The planchette is a heart-shaped piece of wood having two small castors at the base and a pencil inserted through the peak. It is placed on paper and the hand is rested lightly upon it. Providing one is mediumistic in this way, after a while it will move and write intelligently. Many proofs of spirit presence have been conveyed, and there have been published many books of spirit messages received in this manner. Sometimes the planchette will draw intricate designs, faces, and so on, but the value of these is not yet fully known. Our standards are so utilitarian that we are disposed to set on one side anything of which the immediate use is not apparent.

One of the things which is often impressive in these phenomena is the sense of presence conveyed, together with the characteristics of the communicator. This is shown in nearly all these forms of phenomena. A tilting table can convey in a most emphatic manner the peculiarities of the communicator. With the light volatile personality it will move with quick excited motion, while the more staid and solemn communicator is revealed in the sedate and deliberate manner in which the movements are made. This is also manifest with planchette and ouija, and regular users of these can tell at once by the "feel" of the movement who is communicating. There is in all genuine psychic phenomena of this kind this sense of presence, which even those usually unaware of psychic power are able to sense. In assessing values and evidence, the sitter has to take cognisance of this. It is very definite.

It cannot be too earnestly impressed upon the reader that this is not a parlour game, and its practice must not be too frequently indulged in. Until the psychic is completely protected, twice a week is usually sufficient. People sometimes seek to force their way into the next life without preparation or trying to understand anything about the matter. That there are so few casualties is, I think, splendid testimony to the watchfulness of those in the next stage of life. "Fools may rush in where angels fear to tread", but the angels often try to protect the foolish ones, though they will at the same time teach them a salutary lesson.

Automatic Writing

Automatic writing and drawing come under the same rules, but apparatus is discarded. The sitter takes a pencil and, holding it in his hand, relaxes his arm, leaving it free to be used by spirits. At first there will be meaningless scrawls, but after a while words will be written and, as the control of the hand becomes stronger, messages will come through. Very remarkable teachings have been received in this way. *Spirit Teachings*, by the Rev. Stainton Moses, and the *Cleophas Scripts*,* through Miss Geraldine Cummins, are outstanding examples of this kind of writing.

The rules already given apply here also. Care must be taken. The sitter should not play with this power. Over some minds it exercises a strong fascination, and the few cases of obsession that I have met have been due to the sitters exercising this faculty to excess. These faculties are not designed to supersede our ordinary reason, but to be supplementary thereto. The spirit world is not an inquire-within-about-everything sort of burëau. Mediumship is for our help, but not to take the place of our ordinary faculties.

Sometimes the sensitive is entranced, but not in every case. Some mediums engage their minds in reading while their hand is used in automatic writing. This is held to prove that the conscious mind has nothing to do with the messages, but it does not rule out the subconsciousness of the automatist. In the case of Mrs. Piper, there sometimes manifested two personalities at the

*Rider & Co. 3 volumes.

same time, one speaking through her lips, the other using her hand to write. Such complexity of control is very rare.

Why some sensitives must be entranced and others not is probably due to some differences in the organism necessitating that the waking mind has sometimes to be put out of action. Some form of dissociation is necessary for the hand to come under the control of another mind. In cases where trance is necessary, the normal control over the hand is probably too complete for anything to be done until a state of trance is induced and the necessary dissociation obtained. Sometimes the automatist knows what word is being written ; in such cases the automatist is following what is being written and the normal mind receives part of what is coming through. Often, however, the mind will think a word is going to follow what has been written, but to one's surprise another word will be used. It is sometimes a help to watch what the hand is writing, but there is always the danger of suggestion from the normal self interfering with the flow. It is better not to watch too closely, or, if one does, to do so with a passive mind.

Inspirational Writing

The philosophy of inspiration will be dealt with in a later chapter. Here I will give some suggestions for its development. Inspirational writing and speaking differ from both automatic writing and trance control in that the sensitive is aware of all that is being written or spoken. Thoughts stream through the brain without any conscious volition, from some source other than the normal mind of the medium.

People sometimes ask: "How can one know the difference between inspiration and one's normal thinking?" The difference is known mainly by the spontaneity of inspirational writing and speaking. The faculty depends upon the degree of impressibility and receptivity of the sensitive's mind. It is, of course, far more common than is supposed, and most writers have experienced it. In my own case, I find that the inspiration is preceded by a desire to write, though I do not at all times know what the theme will be. This urge is usually felt by those who practise either automatic or inspirational writing. Two of my books, *Altar Lilies* and *The Candle of the Lord*, were written under stress of inspiration. I did not know what theme would be dealt with. Often the inspirer would write in parable. It is an interesting phase and a joy to any who have the faculty.

This form of writing is often accompanied by an awareness of another presence; there is an overshadowing which is so vivid that one cannot doubt the presence of someone unseen. The sense of companionship at such times is very real and often comforting and refreshing. Under stress of inspiration the rate of writing is speeded up; indeed one has to go at top speed to keep pace with the flow of thought. There is some slight departure from the normal state, for when one has completed the writing and goes over it, it is as fresh as something that has been written by another. Sometimes the inspiration is by a slight audition, as of a voice inside one's head speaking the sentences very softly.

To develop the power of inspirational writing, it is wise to set apart a definite time, say two or three times a week. The would-be medium should not be physically weary, and the brain should be clear and not filled with the cares of the day. Sit passive and wait for the words. If one has the power it will soon manifest. Don't wait until the whole thought is clear; write what comes into the mind. If you begin a sentence and do not know how it will end, never mind, go on; your job is to record, and not to bother unduly about the formation of sentences, though of course one must observe the rules of grammatical construction.

If the inspirer has lived in some far-off time, the language and construction of sentences may reflect an earlier age. If that be so, the work, if good, will repay recasting in a more modern form. Often the reception of messages in this way is accompanied by a mental glow, a feeling of warmth and well-being, which at times rises to a mild ecstasy and exaltation of mind; a sense as of being lifted out of one's self. The creative powers of the mind are stimulated to an unwonted degree and, while in that state, whatever is written is invested with meanings which others may not be able to see, and which the writer himself may lose on coming to himself. One thing has to be noted in this kind of writing: that is the tendency to verbosity, the over-generous use of superlatives.

The wise will always go over what has been written and prune it; the blue pencil must be used. Often out of a thousand words it will be found that the message can be reduced by at least a third, sometimes by one half; and yet the essential strength and beauty of the original script can be preserved. Unfortunately, many who receive messages regard them with undue reverence, and think they must not be altered. How much we might have been spared if all recipients of inspiration had exercised their critical faculty instead of being hypnotized with the wonder of the process! Much that has been published would never have seen the light, and the authors would have saved their money, and the tempers of many irate readers. However, it is natural to regard what comes through one's own mind as authoritative.

Inspirational speaking is like writing, but the message is delivered orally. The sensitive becomes conscious of an overshadowing presence, and a stimulation of the emotions. At times a state of light trance is induced, in which the speaker, while knowing all that is said, will have no recollection of it when the message is completed. It can be likened to a dream. For the development of inspirational speaking it is best to try to get into a good circle where something of the processes are known. Inspiration is usually clearer where the inspired one is of a studious mind, reads wisely, and is critical of what comes through. Great orators are often inspired, and the moving passages in many a speech owe their origin to this power.

Clairvoyance

This literally means clear-seeing: the ability to respond to a wider range of vibrations than is usual with normal vision. There are two degrees of this faculty, the objective and the subjective. In the former the visions are seen as plainly as other objects in space; in the latter they are seen as pictures which rise in the mind. This latter phase is more common than is supposed, for people put down to imagination things which are really manifestations of incipient clairvoyance. The difference between imagination and clairvoyance is that the former is the result of conscious effort, the latter is not. In one case the power of the mind is used consciously, in the other the images rise spontaneously in the mind. The veridical nature of these images can be tested; often they are accompanied by a sense of vivid reality, a clear sentience in which the seer partially enters into the disposition of the image of the person seen. People sometimes experience this and consider it strange, or peculiar, but not having any knowledge of psychic matters are not aware it can be developed, and in some degree systematized.

As with automatic writing, some use simple apparatus to evoke the faculty, such as a crystal, a spot of ink in the palm of the hand, a glass of water, or some black surface. Some advocate the training of the visualizing faculty. Thus they say: "Look at some simple object, get as vivid an impression as possible; then close the eyes and endeavour to see it mentally." With practice one may be able at a later stage to project the mental image and see it as an objective reality. Some people can do this, and some artists are able to recall the impression of a sitter with such vividness as to paint from the image they see. While this is a form of clairvoyance, it does not necessarily mean that one will become responsive to higher rates of vibration. It is more in the nature of mind-training than actual clairvoyance.

The object of a crystal (or other means), is that it provides a point for the concentration of vision; it also induces mild hypnosis. The crystal should be placed so that no shadows fall upon it. It is usual to wrap a black cloth around it and gaze into its depths as into a deep pool. If there is any clairvoyance the crystal will become cloudy and milky in appearance. This will clear and images of people or scenes will appear. Sometimes these scenes will be of one's past life, and occasionally a projection of future events. Some people place a lighted candle behind the crystal and gaze through it at the flame. Whatever method is pursued the results will be the same. By gazing into the depths of some black object, such as ink in the palm of the hand or in a saucer, a state is induced in which the gazer is able to see visions. How the images come, and are objectivized in the crystal or ink, is not known. Whether the power is one residing in our sub-consciousness, or whether the source of the visions is in another mind, is a matter for discussion. What we do know is that by these simple means clairvoyance can often be developed.

But the majority of clairvoyants do not use outside aid. Usually one finds they work in conjunction with those whom they call their "guides". Guides are spirits associated with mediums to help in their work. From observations, it seems to me that in such cases the sensitive is in a state of slight hypnosis induced by the guide, who is able telepathically to transfer to the mind of the sensitive what he receives or sees. For the development of this form of clairvoyance the friendly home circle is the best. (See previous chapter.)

The visions often begin as mere impressions and the would-be clairvoyant should describe any impressions received; they will often be recognized by some sitter. The rules already given apply here also.

Many are apt to think that what the clairvoyant sees is an objectivation of what is already in the mind of the sitter. If that be so, why is it that in the majority of cases the descriptions are of people of whom one is not thinking? If it is the reading of the sitter's mind, one would expect that what was uppermost in his mind would be described. It seems that there is a deliberate attempt on the part of someone unseen to disabuse the sitter as to the matters being merely telepathic impressions received by the medium from his mind.

CLAIRAUDIENCE

This often accompanies clairvoyance; it means clear-hearing. In this state the sensitive audibly receives names of people and messages. He hears them spoken, and when well developed the faculty can be of great assistance. The best and most successful clairvoyants are those who have a well-developed power of clair-audience. A difficulty which most sensitives have, however, is that of regularizing and stabilizing the faculty. Some receive strings of Christian names, many of which do not apply to the listener. Every sensitive should strive to come to an understanding with his spirit-helper. Often the co-operation is not as close as it should be. If the guide can get Christian names, why not surnames? One cannot help having the impression of slackness. Perhaps the guide thinks: "That is enough for them."

That some clairaudients and clairvoyants do get full names is evidence that more might be done by others. Some are content with the mere wonder of being able to see and hear, and make no real attempt to get the best. Of course, much depends upon the virility and extent of the faculty; all are not mediumistic geniuses; but as in the case of music, for instance, the player who patiently practises is able to perform well, while one who has better talent but does not practise will only play indifferently. Every sensitive should strive to get into intimate association with his guide, and if the guide is slack or remiss he should be admonished and requested to do better.

In all these matters one should strive for mastery, to be as much as possible above conditions. The voices that are heard are not objective; they fall on the inner ear, sometimes being only vivid impressions. One "listens in" to the voice, which conveys matters of an evidential rather than a philosophical or religious nature, as is the case in inspiration. For public work evidence is essential, and it should be as complete as possible.

Psychometry

This is a very interesting faculty of the mind. The word means soul-measuring; it is the ability to read, from mere contact with objects, something of their history or of that of the people who have handled them. With regard to psychometry, the theory is advanced that everything has an atmosphere which is able to retain the impressions of surroundings and happenings which take place within their vicinity. Some of the hauntings of which one hears are probably due to the psychic atmosphere of buildings having been saturated with the violent emotions of some person who lived in them.

These, retained in the aura of the house, become revivified by any who may be psychic (for it is not everyone who becomes conscious of such hauntings. Of course, this does not apply to those cases where the haunting is not psychometric, but is due to the presence of some earth-bound soul.)

The psychometric faculty is used by everyone, though it is not generally recognized as such. Why, when we approach a stranger, do we "feel" either attracted or repelled? Before we speak or shake hands we may have summed him up. We have received an impression, and often that impression is a warning which we ignore to our future disadvantage.

For the development of this faculty, sit comfortably and take the object, which may be a letter, lock of hair, photograph, ring, or other article (not silk), and hold it in the hand with the tips of the fingers upon it; or it may be placed on the forehead. If the faculty is active, impressions will arise in the mind, or definite sensations will be registered. It is a sound rule to give out what one senses either as impression or sensation, no matter how trivial or foolish, as it may convey a definite meaning to the owner of the object. If after a few impressions have been received a blank should ensue, stop the experiment. Nothing can be achieved by trying to force matters.

If possible, have regular times for experimenting, and do not carry on when very tired, nor extend the sitting to the point of exhaustion; always close with some reserve of power still remaining. As the faculty strengthens, the impressions will increase in intensity until one becomes, for the time being, one with the influences emanating from the object. Remarkable results are often achieved, and this faculty is one which could be used for the detection of criminals who elude the police.

The psychometrist must exercise discrimination. Often what is first received are the surface impressions of the sub-conscious mind of the sitter. Most people have their little romances, avenues of escape from the drab world of everyday. The psychometrist often senses these impressions and is apt to give them to the sitter in the form of prophecy. Certainly it gives hope, but the disillusionment is very disappointing. An endeavour should be made to get to the fundamental influence of a sitter's life, then a true reading will be given.

This faculty can, in some cases, be used for diagnosing disease. Some doctors possess it, and it is rumoured that a few make use of psychometrists to help them in their work. When a psychometrist is able to diagnose he often gets impressions of a remedy, for in this as in all mediumistic work the sensitive is not working alone. There is a spirit helper in attendance upon him who assists him in separating the lines of influence.

This faculty has been tested so often, and the results have been so amazing, that it is certain we shall hear more of it as time goes on.

One form of it is known as water divining. Some people are susceptible to the influences streaming from the waters and minerals in the earth, though they may be unaware of the faculty until their attention is directed to it. One of the peculiarities of psychic work is that when the mind is concentrated on it, it arouses the latent faculty. So with the diviner who, experimenting with his forked hazel-twig held firmly in his hands, finds as he walks over the ground that when he passes over any spot where there is water, the twig turns in his hands, sometimes so violently as to break it. Often he can tell at what depth the water is and what will be the yield. This is so well known that governments sometimes make use of diviners to find water in districts where it is needed.

Healing

Many may not regard the healing of the sick by the laying on of hands as a form of mediumship, but it is so largely used by Spiritualists that it must be considered as a form of psychic activity. There are various forms of healing, such as magnetic, mental, and spiritual healing. The basis of all these is that man is a spiritual being. In this they differ from medical science, which is materialistic, seeking the cause of disease in the physical body.

Some healers affirm that there is only one disease—an interference with the flow of the spiritual forces in the body; thus all diseases are but symptoms of the one disease. Those who employ these forms of healing regard the body as the manifestation of spirit, and not itself a cause of disease; as, apart from the spirit, body has no life. Health of body depends upon the power of the spirit to keep its forces flowing freely through the body. There are factors, such as heredity, which have to be considered, but even so, when traced back, it is seen that health depends upon the individual; that he himself has set in operation the causes which produce either good or bad health. Thus the healer directs his efforts to the establishing of the flow of spiritual forces throughout the body.

Magnetic healing is accomplished by the healer laying

on his hands, or making passes over the affected part. It is based on the idea that health is as catching as disease. By these methods the healer is able to transfer vitality from his own to another body. This vital force is sometimes so strong that I have known it to make percussive sounds around the patient. The magnetic healer is often mediumistic, and works in collaboration with some spirit who impresses on him how and where to make the passes. The magnetic healer is one whose system generates more vital force than he needs. If he acts wisely he does not suffer from depletion, but if he exercises his gift when not in perfect physical condition, he is unable to do any good to his patient, and will often do harm to himself. Many people possess this power but are unaware of it. It is one that has been used from ancient times and has been known in all ages.

The passes are usually made from the brain down over the body, the object being to get the nerve forces to flow freely while at the same time the healer reinforces those of his patient. Generally, the magnetic healer is so much *en rapport* with his guide that he knows intuitively what kind of pass to make for the complaint he may be treating. Here I can only hint at the method ; to go into the treatment of every disease would require a volume to itself.

The mental healer does not use passes, but relies upon the power of suggestion. Based on the theory that mind is superior to the body, one has only to affirm health to attain it. While theoretically sound, it is not always borne out in practice, the success of the mental healer being dependent upon the suggestibility of his patient. It is a good thing to give the suggestion silently. The tendency for most of us, if suffering, is to refuse any suggestion that we are well. If the waking mind is not active and knows not what is being suggested to the sub-conscious, the suggestion can get by it and arouse the sub-conscious to action. This is not mediumship in the ordinary accepted term, but as it forms part of the methods of all healers, I mention it in passing.

Spiritual healing differs from magnetic healing only in that the healer does not rely upon his own vital force, but holds himself as a channel for the transference of health from the inner planes of life. Like the magnetic healer he makes use of passes, and for such healers a knowledge of how to make the appropriate passes is essential. Many who are not very impressionable, and are more dependent upon a knowledge of technique than the magnetic healer, use this method of healing. The use of the method does tend to develop an increased sensibility, so that often there is a blend of the magnetic and the spiritual methods. As a matter of fact, it will be seen that those who have magnetic power are the most successful healers and get quicker results, no matter what method is used.

The spiritual healer puts himself in a receptive attitude so that he becomes a channel for the transmission of the healing power. For this he must be able completely to surrender himself to the higher powers—in the words of religion, to God. While treating a patient he exists only to transmit the divine life, to be the channel through which it may flow to the sufferer. Any thoughts that he is doing the work himself immediately set up a barrier, and the patient does not receive any help. The healer must learn completely to abandon himself to God, to regard himself merely as an instrument of the Divine. Humility is one of his greatest assets, for when pride comes in, the power to heal goes out. To heal the sick, comfort the sorrowing, and restore confidence to weakened minds is one of the greatest works of all. But one must be worthy ; self-seeking will prevent any great success.

The would-be healer will find that a knowledge of the anatomy of the body is necessary. He should know something of the nervous system, of the circulatory system, and the functions of the various organs of the body. He should also ally himself to some responsible healer who can train him in the methods, so that he may acquire a knowledge of the necessary technique, but he should not slavishly follow any system, but should hold himself at liberty to exercise his own intuition. Individuals differ, and if the healer feels impressed to depart from accepted methods he should do so, taking care to watch results and note what happens. By such means he will enlarge his own knowledge and increase his sphere of usefulness.

It will be seen then that, in all mediumistic work, the sensitive should be animated with lofty ideals, should strive for the highest, and not be content with low standards. Given this, and a reverent spirit, he will find the exercise of his powers a blessing to himself and to others.

CHAPTER V

THE DEVELOPMENT OF MEDIUMSHIP—*continued*

Materialization—Direct Voice—Apports and Telekinesis—Levitation and Transportation—Slate-writing—Matter Through Matter—Psychic Photography—Supernormal Painting and Drawing—Transfiguration.

MATERIALIZATION

THIS phase of mediumship usually develops from some more simple form. Probably every physical medium has potential materializing power, but few seem capable of supplying it in a sufficient quantity for the building up of complete forms. Every physical medium supplies the ectoplasm necessary for such effects as the movements of objects, raps, spirit lights, direct voice, apports, psychic photography, levitation, and slate-writing.

As materializations are built up by discarnate entities who have a knowledge of the work, it is wise for the would-be materializing medium to pay attention to the advice of the guides. This kind of mediumship does not develop very rapidly, and those who have the power will need the patience to sit for some time, even though nothing happens. It must be borne in mind that a lot of preparation is needed on the inner planes before the manifestations take place. Some of the best mediums had to sit in séances for years before their powers reached any degree of effectiveness. I know of one medium who sat for two years before anything happened. In the early days of the Spiritualist movement people seemed more ready to wait—they were not so impatient as we today, who are affected by the rage for speed, even in the finer things of life.

If one has materializing powers, the guides will announce it. If possible a room should be kept for the purpose. This may not always be convenient, but whenever possible it is a good rule to observe. As the development of this form of mediumship is quicker in darkness, means of excluding light may be adopted. It is wisest, however, for the medium to develop in the light, even though it takes a little longer. A ruby light, sufficient to see objects, is best. If no light is used, the medium should have luminous bands around his wrists and ankles. For materializations, a cabinet in which the medium sits is used. A cabinet can be made by curtaining off a corner of the room.

Some means of checking the movements of the medium should be devised. Tying the medium may, in the early stages of development, hinder the phenomena. As the power increases and the influence over the medium deepens, it may be advisable to fasten the sensitive to his chair so that he will not be tempted to simulate phenomena. This should be done to protect the medium, for though he may be honest, yet when he is in the trance, which is usually necessary for this kind of phenomenon, he is susceptible to the suggestions and thought-currents of the sitters. Naturally, sitters desire to see a form ; their whole minds are centred on this, and the medium is the centre towards which this desire is directed. Under the stimulus of their unconscious suggestion he may be induced to simulate materialization; therefore, any would-be medium for this type of phenomena *will, for his own safety, demand that he be secured so that he cannot respond in any physical way to the strong mental current of the sitters.*

While the medium must be protected, the sitters also have a responsibility. The tendency of many sitters is to regard psychic phenomena as they do those of everyday life. It has been observed that where sitters have taken care to prepare themselves the manifestations have been very much stronger. In one circle, with George Spriggs as the medium, the sitters adopted a non-flesh diet, gave up alcohol and smoking, bathed before the séance, and donned special garments used only when séances were held. They were rewarded, for on one occasion the spirits materialized so completely that one of them accompanied a member of the circle down the garden to the green-house and picked a bunch of grapes, which he took back and gave to the sitters. This reveals the possibilities. The sitters gave the best conditions they could, and the spirits responded so well that when materialized their forms were as real as those of the sitters.

Of course, sitters should not grab any form. A certain type of mind is so engrossed with its own acuteness that mediums are sometimes exposed to the ignorant methods of the egotistical sceptic. Such sitters usually get what they take to séances, and while they may be loud in their condemnation of the medium, they should condemn themselves, as in all probability they are responsible for the sensitive's lapse from grace. If it is sometimes necessary for sitters to be on their guard against the frauds of some would-be medium, it is also necessary for the mediums to be protected from the dishonest tactics of the unscrupulous sitter.

Direct Voice

When developed, this form of mediumship is of great value. By its means spirits are able to speak to their friends as if face to face. As in the case of materialization, darkness has been found to be an aid in developing it, though some of the best direct voice phenomena have occurred in the light. It can be developed so that spirits can speak in the light, and this should be the aim of the medium. Darkness as a condition is regarded—and rightly so—with suspicion. It is found that the use of a trumpet is a help. These can be purchased at any of the psychic centres. The trumpet acts as a megaphone, though at times the spirits will speak without it. It is not uncommon for two or more voices to be heard at the same time speaking to different sitters.

Here again we are dependent upon the influence of the unseen operators. As we have seen, mediums are attended by "guides" whose work it is to assist in the production of phenomena, to direct proceedings, and protect their sensitives. Those who advance to the stage where the direct voice is possible will do well to observe the advice given by their guides.

When sitting for this form of phenomena, the members of the circle should meet at an appointed time. If necessary, light can be excluded, but a ruby light is advisable. The medium need not be in a cabinet and the sitters should hold hands—this rule should be observed in all dark séances—as sitters can then control one another. The medium can sit amongst the sitters, his hands being held by those on either side of him. The trumpet, which should have a band of luminous paint on the wide end so that its movements may be observed, should be placed in the centre of the circle.

The time can be passed either in singing or light conversation. Manifestations of power will be noted by the spirits trying to move the trumpet. When the voices come through, they will, at first, probably be similar to that of the medium. That is because the power is being drawn from him, and it seems that in some way the medium's larynx is used. As the power increases the voices will develop the characteristics by which they were known on earth. In judging the reality of the phenomenon it is not the voice alone by which it should be judged, but by the matter which is conveyed. The voice may resemble that of the medium, but the message communicated will probably be something known only to one of the sitters. At first the voice may only be able to make some trivial remark, give a name, or merely say "my love" or "remembrance". As the power increases from week to week, it becomes stable and more flexible, so that the spirits are able to manifest at different parts of the circle. An observance of the rules given for materialization will be of help here also.

Apports and Telekinesis

Telekinesis is the movement of objects without any perceptible normal means. *Apports* are objects brought into rooms from a distance. These phenomena indicate that the field of mediumistic activity is much wider than in any of the other forms of psychic happenings. Objects, such as live birds, clay tablets from far-off countries, fishes, etc., are fairly common, while flowers are even more so. The development of this form of mediumship is along the lines already given for materialization and direct voice, with which forms of psychic activity it is allied.

In the production of telekinesis we have that mysterious substance called ectoplasm used for the purpose of moving objects in various parts of the room. The studies of Dr. W. J. Crawford with the Goligher Circle at Belfast indicated that this substance emanating from the medium took on a cantilever form by which articles were moved. The same force is used for tilting a table, only direct contact is not needed. The rules given for the development of physical mediumship for table-tilting stand good here. Indeed, those who can get any object to move by contact can, if patient, usually develop the power to move objects without contact. Often, if the "guides" are appealed to, they will endeavour to develop the power. As already shown, mediums and "guides" are sometimes slack; both need to be encouraged.

It is a good rule in mediumship never to be satisfied with what is attained. It will be found that the higher our demand, the more effective will be our work. Let mediums learn to co-operate more closely with their guides and request them to try and do more than they are accomplishing.

If it is possible for spirits to move an object when the medium is in contact with it, it should be possible for them to move it without the medium in contact. A still further development is to bring objects from a distance. A physical medium supplies that quality of ectoplasm whereby almost any form of physical phenomenon may be produced. Bear in mind that in spirit-life there are those who *have* the necessary knowledge; appeal to them for their help. If you want apports, request that someone should come who has the knowledge of the forces by which they may be brought; if you want movements of objects without contact, again ask those who have the knowledge of how it can be accomplished to come and help. All mediumistic development should be undertaken as a serious study; you will then avoid danger. Do not be flippant; if you are, do not be surprised if you attract spirits of like character who may not merely be flippant, but even malicious.

Levitation and Transportation

This is included in what has already been said above. An object which moves without contact is a levitation. The term, however, is usually applied to the lifting up of the sensitive. I have referred to the classic instance of D. D. Home. Sometimes, accompanying such forms of mediumship, there is an elongation of the medium; that is, his height is increased. This is the opposite of the decrease in form which sometimes accompanies materialization. Levitation is possibly accomplished by the extrusion of ectoplasmic rods which act as levers, lifting the medium into the air. The means of development are the same as for the forms already dealt with.

Slate-writing

For this phenomenon all that are needed are a couple of slates and a grain of pencil. It is not a very common form of mediumship, but may be very convincing. It does not manifest immediately, generally developing from some other form of physical mediumship. The medium sometimes asks the sitter to write a question on one side of a slate, which is then turned over so that the sensitive does not know the question. A grain of pencil is placed on it and the slate is held against the under side of a table. In a few moments a scratching will be heard, and on the withdrawal of the slate an answer to the question will be found to have been written. Sometimes a grain of pencil is placed between two slates and left upon the table while writing is produced. The medium usually finds it necessary to touch the slates with one hand, but not always. The validity of the phenomenon must be judged not alone by the impossibility of the medium producing the writing, but by the evidence of identity conveyed in the message.

Matter Through Matter

This has been touched on in the section on *apports*. These are articles brought into closed rooms. In certain experiments, attempts have been made to get some small article into a locked box. Prof. Zollner, with the medium Slade, was successful in getting such things as the tying of knots in an endless string, the placing of small articles in a locked box, and the placing of wooden rings on a table-leg which were too small to be slipped over it.

I remember an experience with Mrs. Trueman of Plymouth, a personal friend of mine, which was a good example of this form of phenomenon. The séance was held one Sunday evening, after she had been taking the service at the Exeter Spiritualist Society's hall in Market Street. The séance was held in the house of Mrs. Granger, about a dozen people being present.

Acting on one of those impressions which sometimes come to me, I waited until everyone had entered the room where the séance was to be held, then, taking off my overcoat, wrapped my soft cloth hat in it, placed it on the stairs, and entered the room. I was the last to enter and no one went out, the door being immediately closed. Mr. Harold Granger sat on a chair with his back against the door. After some interesting phenomena such as the production of spirit lights, one of the sitters, a Mr. Pye, said that something had come into his hand which he thought was a hat. When the séance was over and the gas was lit, it proved to be *my* hat. I immediately went to look at my coat and found it still rolled up as I had left it!

This phase of psychic phenomenon was a common one in Mrs. Trueman's séances. Such an advanced form is a later development of some simpler aspect of mediumship. Its interest is mainly scientific, as it has some bearing on the problems of space and the constitution of matter. It does not prove survival, though it does reveal that some intelligence is acting which has a knowledge of natural laws far greater than any living scientist. Some suggest that this phenomenon is produced by the action of some being living in a fourth dimension, but that does not explain it. No one knows "how" these effects are produced.

The would-be physical medium who is desirous of reaching these interesting stages of development must be patient. He should come to some clear understanding with his guides and request that someone in spirit-life with the requisite knowledge should be appointed to help in the production of the phenomena. It is always wise to act as if there are intelligent operators and treat them as you would friends. The response will be worth it. Let it be, as already stated, a matter of co-operation between medium and guides, and good work can be accomplished. Suspicion and mistrust lead nowhere.

Psychic Photography

This interesting form of mediumship has been, and still is, the subject of much controversy. Much bitterness of spirit has been expressed and hard words said on both sides. One side says it is all fraud ; the other that it is a genuine thing. Like all forms of psychic phenomena which have been duplicated by interested parties, there is a true and a false psychic photography. Wherever you find a counterfeit of anything you know that the genuine article exists.

Psychic photography was first discovered by William Mumler (1861), an engraver who obtained an "extra"—the name by which psychic photographs are known—which strangely enough turned out to be that of a man still in the flesh ! In the eyes of the unsympathetic that was sufficient to stamp it as fraud. Nevertheless, experiments went on, and today psychic photography is a recognized fact. A number of extras of dead people have appeared on plates, of some of whom there is no photograph in existence. No one knows how it is done ; not even those who are mediums for this form of phenomena. All that they know is that in their presence these things happen. We do not even know what are the particular conditions necessary for the spirits to be able to make a picture of themselves appear on a photographic plate.

In producing the phenomenon it is found helpful for the medium to hold the plates, and sometimes it is found helpful if the one desirous of receiving an extra carries the plates on his person for some time before the sitting. This is supposed to charge them with psychic force, which the unseen can use to impress the image upon the plate. The photographs are taken in the usual way. The plates are placed in the camera, the sitter posed, while the medium acts as an ordinary photographer. He may develop the plates, but it is often found that extras appear even when the psychic does not touch them or the camera, the sitter developing the plates himself.

The question whether a really fraud-proof and reliable psychic extra has ever been taken is still disputed by some, but the work of Traill Taylor and others has shown that psychic photography is a genuine phenomenon. Too much notice should not be taken of those critics whose attitude is : "It would not have been so if I had been there." These folks are apt to mistake their egotism for intelligence. It is always easy to criticize a happening at which one was not present. The credulity of the sceptic is worse than that of the believer, and not as reasonable.

If one desires to develop this form of mediumship he should try to get some information from a reliable medium as to whether he has the power. If he is told he has, he can then put it to the test. He must be prepared for many disappointments, and to spend some money on plates and chemicals. Let him approach the experiments with an open mind, and, as always, invoke the help of his spirit guides. He should speak to them as he would to a living person, and request their assistance. If he has the power, it will probably first show on the plates as patches of light. With patience, this will gradually give place to definite pictures of faces.

Skotographs are pictures which appear on plates held in the hand, or placed upon the forehead without being opened or placed in a camera. Many such have appeared, and it is an interesting form of psychic photography. It has been found possible to impress a strongly visualized mental image upon a photographic plate without putting it in a camera. This power usually accompanies the ability to get psychic extras and is an interesting form of the phenomenon.

Supernormal Painting and Drawing

I have already touched on this in the section on automatic writing. It takes two forms, one in which the sensitive draws or paints automatically, and the other in which pictures appear on cards or canvas without the sensitive acting at all, his mere presence being sufficient for a picture to be precipitated by the unseen artists.

David Duguid, who was said to be controlled by Jacob Ruisdael, used to receive his pictures in the dark. They were mostly landscapes, and for many years were a common form of manifestation at his séances. This power sometimes comes suddenly. A person may feel strongly impressed to paint. On acting on the impulse to do so, he finds that he can paint pictures, and some creditable work has been done even though there has been no knowledge of technique. While he is in a highly impressionable state, his hands are guided so that the colours are mixed and the painting completed. This impressionable condition is comparable to trance. He may be quite aware of his surroundings and even of what is being done through him. The rules already given for automatic writing apply here.

Direct painting is more rare. The Bangs Sisters of Chicago were noted mediums for this form of phenomenon. Vice-Admiral Usborne Moore made a long investigation of their mediumship and was convinced of its genuineness. Certainly it is a most interesting experience to see a picture appear before one's eyes in broad daylight. Such a high form of mediumship is naturally developed from some lesser form, and does not manifest in the early stages of psychic unfoldment The general rules already given apply to all forms of mediumship. Any modifications necessary will be revealed to the blossoming sensitive. Like every other power, it varies with the individual, and sensitives must observe the conditions, learn to co-operate intelligently with their guides, and be prepared for any amount of criticism. They are sure to get it.

TRANSFIGURATION

This is really a form of materialization. Instead of the spirits building up an independent form they mould the sensitive's face so that it alters. By this means it is possible for them to fashion a recognizable likeness which can clearly be seen by the onlookers. Often the spirits content themselves with merely producing a likeness of one of the guides. In this form of mediumship the sensitives should impress upon their guides the necessity of producing faces which can be recognized by sitters. The rules already given for materializations will apply here, and if those who have this form of mediumship will be patient and not rush too soon into the light of publicity, it will be a valuable means of establishing the truth of survival.

CHAPTER VI

UNREGULATED MEDIUMSHIP

Poltergeist—Obsession.

POLTERGEIST

POLTERGEIST is the name given to a spirit who manifests in a violent and noisy manner—a rackety ghost. If psychic phenomena are dependent upon some peculiar quality of the human organism which when developed we call mediumship, then the manifestations of Poltergeist must likewise depend upon it. The spontaneous manner in which such occur would indicate that they are based upon an unregulated mediumship, for we do not experience such happenings in the presence of developed mediums. Poltergeists may be regarded as invasions from another realm, and the invaders may be beneficent, mischievous, or malicious; usually they are of the two latter types.

That such phenomena as throwing stones, raining dust upon food about to be eaten, moving and breaking furniture, spontaneous combustion, etc., occur, is borne out by the testimony of many reliable witnesses. Such cases as that at Tedworth in 1661, the hauntings at Epworth in the vicarage of the Rev. Samuel Wesley in

1761, and the ringing of bells in the house at Great Bealings, which lasted for fifty-three days, are but a few of the recorded instances of this kind of spontaneous phenomena.

From time to time the public is regaled with accounts of some mysterious happening of this kind. The usual attitude is to put the thing down to a trick. It is worthy of note that the happenings are associated with some person, usually a boy or girl of about twelve or thirteen years of age. Because the phenomena happen in their presence and cease when they are not at hand, the ignorant conclude that the disturbances are due to trickery. It does not reflect creditably upon the intelligence of those who suffer that they are unable to discover how the trick is done. That children should be able to deceive their elders in this way is a rather ridiculous assertion.

These phenomena take place in all parts of the world, and the native in his grass-hut is afflicted as is the civilized man in his house of brick. Fortunately the phenomena are comparatively rare, and well that it is so, for such a haunting can be a very expensive affair ; there is no means of suing a ghost for damage done to furniture or property.

A feature of these occurrences is that they come and go without any apparent reason. The psychic force is very violent, and not well directed. It is as if those who sport with it are not able to control it properly. The very violence of the manifestations leads to a rapid exhaustion of the power, and after a few days or weeks it dies out ; the visitation ceases and becomes just a curious experience for which no reason can be given. Would those who are the mediumistic centre of these manifestations develop into good physical mediums if taken in hand by those who have a knowledge of psychic happenings? It is difficult to say. The manifestations may be due to the emotional changes which take place at puberty, the time when the potential psychics become the centre of these activities. It is an interesting speculation what may be the relation between these happenings and the budding sexual energies of those affected. Such a question cannot be left to one class of phenomenon, but must be applicable to all forms of mediumship. Here is a new field for the psychologist to investigate.

One of the difficulties of these happenings is that they seem unintelligent, and it is difficult to discover any purpose in them. Are they related to those raps due to an automatic explosion of psychic force which some people experience? In some cases of Poltergeist there is evidence of intelligent direction, and sometimes a revengeful spirit takes this means to "get his own back" as we say. He certainly causes annoyance and suffering.

Usually when a Poltergeist commences his racket people are attracted out of curiosity. There is rarely any effort made to treat the matter in an intelligent way. People simply wonder. If the spirit manifesting is vain and fond of notoriety, he will probably produce a number of spectacular psychic tricks (which may be regarded as conjuring on the psychic plane), just to mystify the crowd. Any attempt to get into touch with the one causing the disturbances is rarely considered. That there may be behind the phenomena an intelligent being open to reason does not seem to occur to people. This should be borne in mind and an effort made to get into touch with the disturber.

It is well to bear in mind that one should not fear these

powers. They rarely harm people, and this seems to indicate that there is some restraining force which keeps them from committing injury to persons. In any such cases a quiet, confident, and prayerful condition of mind is the best means of approach. If the Poltergeist is appealed to, he will usually listen to what is said. Some effort should be made to open communication with the spirit. This should be possible through the usual code. Instead of looking on the phenomena with gapes of astonishment, it is wise to make an intelligent attempt to track down the disturber, to get him to communicate and to listen to reason. It may well be that it will be found he is not aware that he is causing so much disturbance, and once he realizes the pain he is causing, he will probably withdraw and leave the household in peace.

The presence of a developed medium would be of distinct advantage in such cases, especially one gifted with clairvoyance. Communication would more readily be opened, and the medium's guides would be a restraining influence and would, in the case of an obstinate Poltergeist, get help from spirits in the higher realms to remove the disturber. Exorcism by a priest does not always act. Much of the effectiveness of a service of exorcism depends upon the psychic qualities of the exorcist. With a developed medium, it will be found that the disturbances can be quickly and effectively stopped.

Sometimes the haunting is due to some spirit acting from motives of revenge. In such cases one must reason with him, point out the unfairness of using such methods, and reveal to him that there is a higher life before him. Show to him the temporary nature of any satisfaction he may be getting, and how the reactions will be painful to himself. When the matter is put before the invader in a clear light he usually sees the wisdom of ceasing his persecution.

It is sometimes considered that the disturbances are due to the action of non-human sources; that is, to nature-spirits, or elementals. The evidence goes to prove that it is usually human spirits who are the cause. If any disturbance takes places through elementals, the presence of a medium and the invoking of higher powers will result in their removal. In all such cases a calm, quiet confidence is essential; fear is apt to increase the disturbances. Remember that the spirit worlds are realms of law and order. Finally, do not ignore the power of prayer.

Obsession

Among spiritualists, opinions differ about the reality of spirit obsession, a few contending that it does not exist, while many affirm its reality. The fact of spirit-control, admitted by all spiritualists, indicates that obsession is possible. There are many cases on record which prove that obsession is a fact. Professor Hyslop, a well-known psychical researcher, writes in his book, *Life After Death*: "Before accepting such a doctrine [obsession] I fought against it for ten years after I was convinced that survival after death was proved." So impressed was he with the reality of obsession that he left a large sum of money in his will to establish a foundation for its treatment. The headquarters for this work is in New York, with Dr. Titus Bull as director.

The work of Dr. Carl Wickland is well known. His

two books, *Thirty Years Among the Dead* and *The Gateway to Understanding*, give the results of his experiences and his method of treatment. In this work he is helped by his wife, who is a good trance medium. The method is as follows:

A charge of static electricity is passed through the patient. This is said to have the effect of driving out the obsessing entity. The spirit is then induced by Mrs. Wickland's spirit-guides to control her. By this means Dr. Wickland is able to reason with the spirit, and induce him to leave the patient. Often it is found that the spirit has not realized he has left his physical body, nor can he tell why he has become entangled in the aura of another person. After being enlightened his vision clears, he becomes aware of the presence of other spirits, and he is taken away from the borderland to the spirit-world; thus both the obsessor and the obsessed are liberated.

What is obsession? It is the domination of the mind by some spirit, or the confusion by close association, which influences the patient's organism, causing suffering both of body and mind. Often the diseases from which the obsessing spirit has suffered in the body persist as a strong memory, and there is a sympathetic reaction in the body of the one obsessed, so that he feels he is suffering from the same complaint. The possibility of this is clear to those who have had any experience of psychometry. Often, in giving a reading, the psychometrist feels the conditions of the person whose aura he is reading.

Obsession differs from possession as occurs in trance mediumship in that the patient is conscious of the division in his mind; he often feels he is two people.

In trance possession the sensitive is usually unconscious. An obsessed person may be aware of the influence of another entity ; sometimes he hears voices, occasionally speaking foul language which distresses him ; he may be the recipient of vile suggestions against which he struggles in vain. There is a sense of divided personality—a consciousness of being invaded by some foreign influence. This condition often results from shock, nervous strain, or organic lesion, low morality and selfish living.

Among spiritualists, obsession is comparatively rare, for in this matter knowledge is a protection. Indeed, the rational development of mediumistic power is the best guard against obsession. To avoid Spiritualism because of the possibility of obsession is no protection whatever. Fear opens the mind to attack. Remember the story of the man who met the Demon of Cholera. Asking him where he was going, the Demon said: "To yonder town." "And how many will you slay ?" asked the man. "A thousand people," said the Demon. Some time after, the man met the Demon again and remonstrated with him, saying : "You said you would kill only a thousand persons, while ten thousand have died." "Quite so," said the Demon. "I killed a thousand ; fear killed the rest."

The moral is plain. As in the case of disease, so with obsession ; a self-possessed person who maintains rule in his own household (body) will not be obsessed. I believe that cases of obsession arise usually outside the ranks of spiritualists.

What can be done to help those who are obsessed to get free from their suffering ?

First, we must be sure that the obsession *is* that of a spirit. Not every case in which the individual hears voices is due to spirits, nor is every case where the individual constantly reverts to some overmastering idea. If it is obsession by a spirit, the one obsessed should strive to reason with him. He should use all possible means to improve his general health. A thoroughly healthy person is seldom obsessed. If the spirit obsessing him will not listen to reason, the aid of someone who has the power to exorcize should be sought. In treating such cases, some dip their hands in water and make the sign of the cross in the air at the back, side, and front of the person obsessed. This is said to be visible in the ether and to act as an S O S to those in the higher realms. It does not always act. A well-developed medium with powerful guides will be more effective. Many good spirits are ready to help in such cases, and with a powerful medium a cure may be quickly effected.

If the obsession is due to too great an absorption in psychic matters, or the unwise use of the planchette, or too free an indulgence in automatic writing, the patient should be induced to drop all studies of this nature ; to go much into the open air and to seek to live a more balanced and rational life.

Prayer can be of great help, and many cases of obsession and haunting yield to it when treated by some prayer-group acting from a distance. I know this from practical experience, having helped a few to become free from this trouble by means of absent-healing. The field of action for absent-healing is unlimited ; distance is no barrier ; a patient can be as easily treated at the other end of the earth as easily as in the same town as the prayer-group. Often when a patient is treated in this way he becomes temporarily worse. This is due to the obsessing spirit struggling to retain his hold on the patient, who reacts so that he appears to be getting worse. After a short but sharp struggle the obsessing entity is ejected and the patient becomes normal. Being freed from his obsession he is clothed in his right mind. This has been experienced by many, and it cannot be accounted for on the grounds of coincidence. No person who is at all psychically sensitive can take part in any absent-healing service without being aware of the powerful influences generated and radiating from it.

The following advice from Dr. Peebles' work, *Demonism of the Ages*, is worth repeating :

> If a person is conscious of troublesome, obsessional influence, if invisible familiars haunt, converse with them. Tell them frankly they are injuring you. Then change your environments. Seek some mountainous district, where the air is pure ; avoid all promiscuous spirit circles ; keep the thoughts upon things moral and spiritual, observe all hygienic habits, and pray for divine help.

If these fail, then seek the aid of someone who has a knowledge of these matters.

Occasionally the obsession may be due to some spirit anxious to develop a sensitive. In such a case a rational development of the sensitive's mediumship will result in a cure. It should not be supposed that we are surrounded by demons seeking to destroy us. That is a theological bogey to frighten children. Such an idea is a strong predisposing cause of obsession.

As more rational ideas of the future life become more widely known, and the misty and vague teaching of the churches about the after-life is replaced with definite knowledge, obsession will become more and more rare. Ignorance is the great enemy in this as in all other things. Pay no attention to those who declare mediumship is evil, that Spiritualism is satanic and will unbalance your reason. The facts are against that view. Ignorance is a danger, not a protection. If the reader will follow the advice in this volume he will have nothing to fear. Speaking from over forty years' experience, I can say that Spiritualism, when rightly understood, is one of the greatest blessings ever given to man. It has comforted millions of aching hearts, given certainty in the place of mere hope, and rescued from grief many on the brink of madness or worse. The obsessing spirits are not all evil, and many of them, if they had had the knowledge of after-death states which Spiritualism gives, would never have remained near the earth and thus become the victims of ignorance.

CHAPTER VII

A WORD TO THE WISE

Séance-room Appointments—A Word to Would-be Mediums—A Word to Sitters.

SÉANCE-ROOM APPOINTMENTS

WHENEVER possible a room should be set apart for the holding of séances. A room set apart and used for séance work only becomes charged with "power", so that the power generated in one séance is conserved and increases as the séances proceed. As a musical instrument by frequent playing becomes more mellow through the atoms of its materials gradually becoming polarized, so does the furniture of a séance-room gradually come to respond to the vibrations of psychic activities.

The furniture need not be elaborate. One corner of the room may be curtained off to form a cabinet, and a plain wooden chair be placed in it for the use of the sensitive. All the chairs should be plain and not upholstered. There should be a table with a shaded lamp, and a writing-pad and pencil for the recording of talks with the spirits or any phenomenal happenings, a trumpet for direct voice, a planchette or ouija board for writing, and a crystal for help in developing clairvoyance. The floor may be either stained or covered with a plain lino.

A small table for telekinetic phenomena and a camera for psychic photography may also be provided if thought necessary.

Some find incense a help in harmonizing the conditions. The wide use of incense in churches is based on the fact that its use often makes psychic manifestations easier ; it has a decided effect upon our finer bodies. A musical box or gramophone is also a help in promoting the emotional state necessary for good work. The light used should be one that can be regulated. Darkness is rarely essential and should not be encouraged ; except for certains forms of physical phenomena, it is not absolutely needed. Remember that the majority of séances take place in the light. A few pleasing pictures may be hung, but are not essential Once the sitters have their appointed places they should keep them, as any change of position entails a rearrangement which may hinder the rapid development of phenomena.

A Word to Would-be Mediums

Do not seek the development of psychic powers out of mere curiosity ; it is a serious study only to be undertaken with pure motives and a desire for the highest.

Do not mistake motives of vanity for altruism. Be sure that it is the desire to serve which actuates you, and not the desire to wield unusual powers. Many people's vanity masquerades as altruism ; by and by the cloven hoof appears and the sensitive goes down at the first temptation.

Always live rationally ; do not seek to exercise your

powers at any and every time of the day. Be as regular in the exercise of your mediumship as in the performance of other duties.

"Try the spirits" : do not accept any control who may wish to use you. A man is known by the company he keeps on the psychic as well as on the physical plane.

Do not think the development of mediumship means that the necessity for study and self-improvement has come to an end ; often it has only just begun.

Remember that an ignorant medium can be a danger. "If the blind lead the blind they will fall into the ditch together." The wider the sensitive's knowledge, the better trained his mind, the more effective will be his work.

Do not indulge in stimulants, nor excessive smoking. Anything which interferes with the proper functioning of the body hinders the right expression of the psychic nature.

Keep the mind calm and poised. Cast out fear and cultivate a loving heart. Regard your spirit-guides as helpers and friends whose advice and counsel should be considered, but do not make them a substitute for your own judgment. Spirit guides should be regarded as friends, not crutches to help you to walk.

Submit all teaching that may come to you to your reason. Do not accept anything on the authority of anyone either in or out of the flesh. Truth alone must be the final authority, and that you have to discover for yourself. If the teaching appeals to you as good and helpful, accept it, and *live* it. Mere acquiescence in a body of teaching is not enough. There are plenty of believers; what the world needs are doers.

Finally, remember that mediumship is a sacred office, the one and only original priesthood of God. Regard it as such, and by daily prayer and meditation seek to become a medium for the highest.

A Word to Sitters

Do not go to a séance with a mind full of prejudices; be reasonable in your expectations.

Treat the spirit people as you would those of earth; be courteous, gentle, and sympathetic.

Don't ask too many questions, as for some reason which we have not yet discovered this seems to cause a congestion and prevents the free flow of the influence. Have patience; it will be found that evidence emerges in a natural manner in general talk.

Keep a note of what is said; it will often be found on reading your notes that a great deal more has come through than you thought.

Do not regard the spirit people as substitutes for your own reasoning power; they like you to think for yourself.

Do not consult mediums on trivial matters. We are here to grow and develop. Learn to use your own intelligence.

Guidance always comes to those who "wait upon the Lord". Learn to make use of silence.

Do not attend séances in a suspicious or fault-finding frame of mind. If you look for fraud you may find it—but it may be your child, not the medium's!

A scientific spirit is not inimical to good séance work, but let it be scientific, and not prejudice masked in scientific nomenclature.

Treat the medium as you would a piece of delicate machinery; remember that a fine sympathy is the oil which makes the psychic forces flow readily and smoothly.

Do not mistake emotionalism for religion, nor woolly statements for mysticism. True religion purifies the emotions, and mysticism has its own symbolism which is as definite as any scientific statement.

Finally, be sincere and earnest in your quest. Remember that mediums are but instruments used by higher powers. Listen to what is said, consider, weigh the evidence, and decide according to your own judgment. Remember, "a humble and a contrite heart is acceptable to God", and often brings what cannot be given to the purely intellectual. Keep the intellect as a tool, regarding it as a part of your equipment. Seek the "more excellent way".

CHAPTER VIII

PHILOSOPHY OF INSPIRATION

Inspiration and Religion—Breath a Primary Condition of Life—Physical, Mental, and Spiritual Breathing—Auras—Thought-spheres.

INSPIRATION AND RELIGION

"FOR there is a spirit in man, and the inspiration of the Almighty giveth him understanding." This saying from the Book of Job expresses the importance of inspiration to man. All through the history of religion, emphasis has been laid on inspiration and its power to increase life. Jesus expressed the same thought when He declared: "I come that ye might have life and have it more abundantly", and has not His teaching and example inspired men to deeds of heroic service, and sustained many in days of doubt and darkness ? Through His example men have breathed a new life, inspired by a purer air than that of earth, and have even laid down their lives in His service.

The many sacred writings of the world are held in veneration because they are regarded as being inspired by God. Only the narrow sectarian will deny to members of another faith the same inspiration for their sacred books which they claim for their own. Unfortunately few receive the inspiration which gives understanding, and one of the bitterest struggles in the souls of men is to emancipate themselves from the narrow views of sectarianism.

Throughout the ages the Spirit of God has spoken to man by inspiration. Prophet, seer, and mystic have each received some meed of the divine breath. Inspiration, however, is not confined to the sphere of religion; it is universal in its power and is expressed as much through the scientist as through the priest.

The power of any inspired utterance is its ability to inspire those who hear or read it. Whatever criticisms may be levelled against theological conceptions concerning the Bible, no one can read the Psalms, the Prophets, or the New Testament without feeling the contact of minds that still live in their recorded utterances. It is clear there can be no religion worthy of the name unless it has the power to inspire its adherents. It must be something more then mere emotion; it must have the power to direct the emotion it arouses into definite channels, and it cannot do this unless it gives light through its power to inspire in believers a consciousness that they can gain direct contact with God. This is the claim of every religion and ritual; creed, dogma, priests, are simply mediums through which may be transmitted power from the higher realms. The efforts of the priest are directed to preparing the minds of worshippers to receive the light of a purer world. Once the light is received—and this is inspiration—its power to change our lives is apparent both to ourselves and to others.

Breath a Primary Condition of Life

The word "inspire" means to breathe in, and that presupposes an atmosphere to be breathed. There is a universal inspiration, for all living things breathe, and it is possible that there is, even in the inorganic kingdoms, something which corresponds thereto. To breathe is to live; without the power to breathe, life in the physical body is impossible. Like so many other functions of our being, we accept the fact without thinking of its importance or hidden meanings. This physical fact expresses on a lower plane a process that is going on in every realm. *Inspiration is a universal inbreathing from God.* It is expressed in Genesis in the words: "And God breathed into man's nostrils the breath of life [lives]; and man became a living soul." The initial breath is from God, but continuance to breathe depends upon us.

Marcus Aurelius states: "God is around us like an atmosphere which we may breathe in if we will." There is, however, an automatism which maintains the conditions for life in form. Physically, we do not consciously breathe. When in health, the function of respiration goes on without any awareness on our part; it is only in times of stress or disease that the act of breathing is forced upon our attention. At the end of our life we give up the ghost; we cease to breathe. The importance of this function is seen in the word "spirit", which means breath, suggesting that our being is dependent upon the primal breath—here synonymous with life—for our continued existence.

Physical Breathing

This goes on automatically. There are schools which teach that if we gain control of our breath we can govern the functions of our bodies in marvellous ways. These schools teach that interpenetrating our atmosphere is a finer one, which they call prana, or life.

Readers of Thorp's *Etheric Vision** will be aware of his experiences of seeing fine particles in the atmosphere, and also of how he found them, in some degree, amenable to his will. In theosophical literature we are told about these particles, which are spoken of as "health globules". They are said to emanate from the sun, and it is suggested that when we have long periods of cloudy weather, and do not receive our full measure of these globules, we are then below par. "The globules, on account of their brilliance and extreme activity, can be seen by almost anyone who cares to look, darting about in the atmosphere in immense numbers, especially on a sunny day. The best way to see them is to face directly away from the sun and focus the eye a few feet away, with a clear sky as background. Brilliant as is the globule, it is almost colourless, it may be compared with white light." (*The Etheric Double.* Major A. E. Powell.)

Students may try this experiment for themselves. Do not mistake specks on the eye, which float out of the range of vision, for these globules, if seen, will be like any other objects in space.

There are said to be different kinds or degrees of prana which are coloured violet, blue, green, yellow, orange, dark red, rose-red.

These globules are drawn into the spleen and distributed to the psychic centres of the body. The violet-blue to the throat-centre, green to the navel-centre and abdomen, yellow to the heart-centre. Orange-dark-red

*Published by Rider & Co. 3*s.* 6*d.*

(and some dark purple) to the base of the spine-centre. Rose-red to the nervous system. The reception and distribution of these globules goes on constantly, and certain forms of breathing are directed to obtaining control of the psychic centres of the body, by means of controlling the flow of prana. Breathing exercises form the basis of many systems of health-culture, and there is no doubt that if we can obtain some control of our breathing we shall be able to resist many of those forces which press so heavily upon us. We should learn to breathe to live, and not merely live to breathe, and a few deep breathing exercises in the early morning and at any convenient time during the day is all that need concern us here.

Stand before an open window, hands upon hips, shoulders back, and inhale through the nose slowly and deeply so that the lungs are filled with fresh, pure air. Hold breath while mentally counting four, then exhale, taking care that the lungs are emptied. Do this for five minutes. At the same time think of the air you breathe as the life of God, holding all you need for your physical, mental, and spiritual refreshment. If you can visualize, imagine yourself in a globe of white light, open at the top, into which is pouring divine life and power which is going to every part of your body, carrying in its life current the wholeness of God. Mentally, rest in God. Do not be tense; relax mentally; this is more important than physical relaxation, though that is good; but if you relax mentally, your body will follow your mind. This exercise should give a feeling of poise, buoyancy, and power. Remember you live in God, you can breathe His Life, and this breath can heal, sustain, and give you the power to overcome much nervous strain.

Mental Breathing

There is a "withinness" to our atmosphere, even to prana; it is the Mind of the universe. This Mind is all-pervading. It is the primal source of all inspiration, though this may be mediated to us through many minds. All knowledge is within; and the various systems of education are devices for drawing it out. Its data is without; facts are but symbols of truths. When we perceive the truth which a fact represents, the fact becomes alive; we perceive its relationship to other facts, and so go on to discover the principles which correlate them.

All efforts to progress are means of developing the germ of perfection within the soul. For this purpose we have to learn to breathe mentally. There is an ebb and flow of thought, an inspiring and an expiring of it. We breathe in the primal element, and we give out a more or less finished product. That is, if we *think*. With many people the mental substance simply flows over their minds, not *through* them, and it is unchanged; only upon the lower levels is some change effected in the mental substance, and not always for the best. Thoughts are the germinal centres of things. We clothe them with matter; on their own plane thoughts have a pseudo-life of their own. That is, we give them direction; an intense thought becomes a power, either for good or ill, according to the direction we give it.

When considering the psychological state, we noted how some people are easily influenced by their surroundings, or by what they hear. Such people sometimes become the unwitting instruments of stronger minds, and if we could trace to their real source some of the crimes which are committed, we should be shocked. Very few of us under provocation are above committing, in thought, acts which we shrink from doing in deed. Can we be sure that the elemental to which we have given birth ceases to exist when that which has evoked it has passed ? Or has it gone out into the ocean of thought and influenced some mind temporarily attuned to it ? Jesus was clear about it : what has been committed in thought has been done in our hearts. On the mental plane the deed has been done.

The great difference between mental and physical breathing is that in the latter we must breathe the air wherever we are, whether it be pure or otherwise : in mental breathing we can select what we will breathe. We can, as soon as destructive thoughts rise in our minds, reject them, refuse them lodgment. Control of our mental life is very difficult, but it must be achieved, for the basis of all creation is mental. When Sir James Jeans wrote: "The universe begins to look like a great thought", he indicated that there is mind behind it ; the universe is the thought of God materialized. If the thought of God be so expressed, may we not, as St. Paul says, "be imitators of God" ? And how better gain the strength to do so than by breathing in God as Aurelius suggests ? We might try.

Spiritual Breathing

Spirit is the primary substance from which emanates all that is. God is spirit, He is the Divine Breath which is the substance manifest in all things. As God is spirit, so are we, dwelling in Him. The inspiration which has manifested with such abundance in the religious life of man may be our daily experience. Spirit permeates all. We are IT in manifestation. All the difficulties and trials of life are means which brings to our consciousness this divine truth. Here we may indeed breathe to live in the very highest sense; we can touch the heart of the Eternal; vision and realization fuse into an all-comprehending understanding. Meditation and prayer will become as necessary for us as eating and drinking. We shall take up our religious exercises with a joy and confidence that will be its own reward and its own bliss. Daily meditation on high and lofty themes will open the mind to the light—the light which is the substance of the Father. Dwelling in that, no evil will touch us, however much it may, for a time, affect the body.

Auras

The word aura means atmosphere and, as used by spiritualists, the atmosphere surrounding persons and objects. This has already been referred to.

There are as many kinds of auras as there are planes of being. Generally speaking, we can only sense the etheric and the psychic, though some may become aware of the higher mental and spiritual auras.

The function of the aura is to protect. Many impressions are received through it which rise in consciousness, either as feelings of mental discomfort, unrest, disquietude, or as definite intuition or vision. It is possible by rightly directed thought to surround oneself with an auric shield, and keep out unpleasant or disturbing influences.

The etheric body is a replica of the physical, but it must

not be confused with the soul, which belongs to a higher plane. Our etheric double is perishable and disintegrates with the physical body. When seen clairvoyantly, it is as a well-defined light edging the physical body, in which can be seen fine hair-like lines or rays, which, when the body is healthy, stand out clear and rigid. When any part of the body is affected by disease, the lines droop and look lifeless. Clairvoyant diagnosis of disease can be given by anyone who has learned to discriminate and discern the signs in the health-aura. Some diseases are said to begin in the etheric body. This body is the vehicle of sensation and is connected with the soul-body.

This latter varies in appearance with the development of the individual. It indicates his character and, to the discerning, reveals much of his past, and also gives intimations of the future. It is possible for a person to have a well-developed soul-aura, but a poor etheric one. Health of soul is not dependent upon health of body. How often do we find pure and lofty minds associated with weak and unhealthy bodies! Thus, while the weak, unhealthy body will have a poor health-aura, the soul-aura may indicate fine spiritual advancement.

In the undeveloped man, the soul-aura is undefined in shape, with much red in it. The colours in the aura indicate according to their purity the state of spiritual health. In the undeveloped man the red is coarse and thick-looking; so is the green, being slimy in appearance and snake-like in motion. Any lighter shades, such as orange, will be coarse and hard in texture. The colours are not stable, though they tend to some sort of order, the lighter colours being at the top, the heavier ones around the loins and lower limbs.

The indefinite outline of the aura indicates lack of spiritual development. With such a man the health-aura may be exceedingly good. It does not follow that an undeveloped man is evil; in many cases he is merely unmoral. The aura of the undeveloped man in civilized communities will show more definiteness than that of an uncivilized man, because he brings into play his mental powers. His aura will have the usual browns, greys, reds, with some deep orange and green, and a dash of blue or purple. The aura will be seen to be unstable; it is often a storm-centre.

The aura of the thinker is more orderly in arrangement, refined in colour, and definite in outline. The red is usually clear, indicating energy; the purity of the green showing adaptibility to changes in circumstances; the browns are touched with gold, revealing hope and trust; the orange varies, according to the idealism of the individual, from reddish-orange indicating earthly ambitions, to the pure lemon-flame of the spiritual thinker. This is seen rising from the head, forming a halo. Purple indicates wisdom and understanding; rose-pink refined affections. These are the stable colours in the auras of advancing souls, but many transient shapes are seen, symbols of various kinds, while the band, or group, to which the individual belongs is indicated by a badge in some part of the aura. Like that of the undeveloped man it is rarely at rest; but it is not stormy, its movement is more orderly.

The extent of the aura differs with each one, in some being only a few inches, in others many yards. It is said that some great souls have auras which extend great distances. On the physical side we have our sun whose aura extends for millions of miles. If we look behind the material sun to its spiritual source, we perceive that its physical aura is commensurate with that of the Divine Being in whose life we dwell.

Expansion of aura is some indication of growth, but an unspiritual man may have a large aura, especially if he indulges in psychic practices. "The brothers of the left-hand path" are not deficient in aura, which because of its gravity can be very powerful on the lower planes. They are confined in their action to the area of repulsion in the lower desire-world ; this is the region of sorcery, the realm of inversion and ultimate death.

The aura is also revealed, at times, through the sense of smell. That of an evilly disposed person gives off an odour of putrescence and decay ; the aura of a spiritual person is perfumed and acts as a stimulant to those who are sensitive to it. In the presence of the good we feel restful, that is, if our life is aspiring, but to the evilly disposed the presence of a good man is a rebuke, and they feel uncomfortable. Thus the aura can be seen, felt, and smelled ; but with most people it is only sensed by touch.

We can improve our auras ; by pure living we clarify and improve their colour, and increase their extent and power.

On the higher planes the aura indicates our affinities. It makes life orderly, and as we progress, so do we grow towards higher conditions, and corresponding changes take place in our auras. While the function of the aura is to protect and help us to find our right conditions, it is also a register of our inward states. In the next stage of existence the condition of the spirit is expressed in the soul-body, the light of which reveals the standard of its development.

There are in the aura centres of power, in which the light glows with finer radiance and power. These centres are linked together by fine lines of light which outline the human form. The well-defined aura is usually egg-shaped, but with advanced souls it is seen as rays radiating out to a great distance. The centres of force are active, though more so in some than in others. They link man to the inner kingdoms, gathering the finer forces and distributing them to the physical body, so that the spiritual essences may be kept in circulation.

Auric contact plays an important part in life, especially in all forms of psychic development. For it is through our auras that our friends on the other side act upon us. In our daily life we are influenced and, to some extent, governed by the auric emanations about us. The strong-willed man is one who can direct the currents of his mind to dominate his fellows. Many of the advertisements which proclaim that they will make you strong of will are designed to sell lessons based upon some slight knowledge of occultism, but it can safely be said that the majority of such advertisements are merely bait for fools to nibble. The true Master never resorts to the methods of the world, but seeks by silent yet potent power to aid all who are in need of help.

Just as we breathe the atmosphere of the earth, so may we breathe its etheric and soul-atmosphere. Within this we live, and between us and it there is a constant interchange of energy. By right living we can enrich the aura of the earth, which in turn endows us with greater power. World-auras link the universe into one; by and by science will discover them and their functions. They are finer than the ether of science, but very little is known about them, even in occult circles. Into the aura of the world go all our thoughts and emotional output. If the peoples of the world are disturbed and agitated, the aura of the earth is affected, and this has repercussions in the physical realm. Such a thought may seem a wild speculation, but if we consider the unity of the universe it is not so unreasonable as it seems at first glance.

Thought-spheres

Let us now see the practical application of these thoughts. Going back to our opening theme, inspiration, we can see the importance of what has been stated. There is an all-pervading atmosphere which is fundamental. It is impersonal, but when breathed it becomes charged with our influence, and it can be directed to build up definite thought-spheres around us, an important matter for the would-be medium. Most of us do this unconsciously by our habits of thought, and such thought-spheres may be prisons. Quite a number of people are prisoners in their own minds. There is a great difference between thought-spheres which are the result of prejudice and those which are the result of definite effort. When we realize that progress means gaining control of the thought-currents of the mental realm and rising above the sphere of purely personal interests, we shall take ourselves in hand and try to gain control of our minds.

The course of our mental evolution is generally thus. First, our interests are within the narrow sphere of self; then they widen to the family; thence to village or town, and so to the nation. With many it goes no farther, and we see the limitations of thought to purely national interests in our political life. If we have developed an international consciousness, it will transcend national barriers, and the conception of brotherhood be extended to all peoples. There is sphere within sphere, from that of self, family, town, nation, to the universal, which embraces all life. Here we have the line of evolutionary development, the stages through which the race is passing.

Now what is the difference between one's own thinking and inspiration? It is one of degree. All thinking is pulsation, or breathing, but in our own thinking we give direction to our thoughts. In inspiration we are not conscious of any mental process. For instance, if we write a letter we generally know what we desire to say, and can clothe our thoughts in appropriate language. With inspiration, one sits down and writes without any idea of what is coming. We may tap some strata of thought so that ideas flow into our minds without effort, or we may be inspired by some spirit in telepathic contact with us. In either case we are the channels through which flow ideas, conceptions, thoughts, which will be expressed according to our intellectual development.

Sometimes inspiration is attended with feelings of exaltation and ecstasy. While it lasts, one's whole being is in a glow, as if in a bright, mellow light in which every idea stands out as a thing of beauty. In one sense the inspirational state is analogous to a dream condition, in which the veriest commonplaces appear as divine wisdom. The inspired one needs to exercise discrimination, and not be fearful of a drastic use of the blue pencil.

At times the inspiration transcends the limitations of the sensitive, but it must be remembered that it often depends upon co-operation with some other mind. A very commonplace mind may, under inspiration, produce a thing of beauty; but that is a rare experience.

Inspiration of the psychic kind is unfolded in conjunction with some directing intelligence, which helps the sensitive to keep his mind passive for the reception of its thought. This process is telepathic in character. Those wishful to experience it should try to still their minds, to turn inward to the radiant point of being, and to seek conscious communion with the highest. For this, prayer is the best method for many people. "They that wait upon the Lord shall mount up with wings as eagles." That is, rise to high levels of thought. Aspiration towards the highest brings a corresponding inspiration.

This leads to the peak of inspiration. When the turbulency of the mind has been stilled, and the soul emptied of all that is of earth, there comes a great calm, a sense of resting upon the deep. In this state there is profound darkness, a sense of aloneness. One is absolutely still; every function of the mind is at rest; even consciousness of self has departed.

Then comes the soft, mellow glow of golden light, like the first signs of dawn upon the hills. It steals into one, fills the heart with a great joy, pervades one as a perfect peace. It cleanses, heals, makes new, and thoughts beyond the power of speech fill the mind. Here inspiration and vision become one. The sense of union with God is complete, the real self knows the Father. All sense of separateness is swallowed up in that of union. Individual consciousness expands to total consciousness, yet with no loss of individuality. One knows one lives in God, and thinks God's thoughts with Him. This is the divine inspiration which sweeps away the barriers of race and creedal limitations. It evokes a love which embraces all creation, revealing it as the word of God; His life made manifest. And through it all sounds the harmony of a Perfect Life and Love.

Part Two

THE MEANING OF MEDIUMSHIP

CHAPTER I

BEYOND

The Purpose of Death—The Process of Death—The Reality of the Spirit-life—Spirit Intercourse and Spirit Communion.

The Purpose of Death

The practice of mediumship brings to those who exercise its powers new views of life and death. As we have seen, the manifestation of mediumistic faculty is dependent upon the close co-operation of spirit-guides. This, of course, means that man survives tne change of death, and the proving of such a stupendous truth is bound to modify our views of that last great change.

Death is regarded by many as cessation of existence. When we speak of anything as dead, we imply a finality, that an end has been reached. Birth and death are natural processes, and in the absence of any proof to the contrary, we cannot regard either as due to causes outside the physical world. The fact that we do survive the change of death suggests many planes of life, all inter-related, and helps to show that earthly existence is not a mere fragment but part of a larger whole.

What is the purpose of death ? Life tends to increase its number of forms of expression, and this increases the pressure of competition ; obviously, then, these forms must give way, that others may have a place in the sun. At its lowest aspect, death is a means of making it possible for life to continue its manifestations on this plane. It is only forms which perish ; life never dies. Thus the higher aspect of death is its making it possible for life to advance to finer forms of expression.

Death is not the result of sin ; it is merely an aspect of eternal change. It is part of the process of becoming. It is an essential factor in the development of life. Everything changes. In the organic kingdom there is decay, a slow disintegration of rocks and minerals. As everything is pervaded by spirit, which is living and conscious, we perceive that these processes are not wanton, but orderly, serving some great purpose. Philosophically speaking, nothing is dead; everything has life, and what is regarded as chemical action resulting in decay and disintegration of substance is due to the action of a more positive force—that is, life. Death means an expansion of being, a move forward ; it is a means of growth. We can realize this if we accept the postulate that behind Nature is Living Spirit and that everything is an expression of IT.

Primarily, it is assumed that there was no life on this planet ; that in course of time life manifested in a form recognizable by science. But even then it is complex, for the simplest form of life, the uni-cellular organism, is simple only in being a single cell—its constituents are complex. It is a very wonderful creature, being in fact the foundation of all others.

The vegetable kingdom is rooted in the mineral ; through its roots the plant absorbs the moisture and salts in the earth, and through its leaves takes from the air and sunlight the gases necessary for its being. It transmutes them ; it raises the apparently lifeless to the kingdom of life. In turn, the plants give food to animals, birds, fishes, and these raise the life of the vegetable another stage. Here we see a slow but continuous advance ; each step forward means the *death of form,* but the *life* does not perish—it goes on to a higher level of manifestation. To quote one of old : "I died to the mineral and became a plant ; I died to the plant and became an animal ; I died to the animal and became a man. Wherefore should I fear death ? When did I become less by dying ?"

From this we see that death is not, as some suppose, the result of sin, but is a process necessary to the continued expansion of life. It is not something to be feared, but, when it comes naturally, to be welcomed as a deliverer from the limitations of earthly existence.

The Process of Death

The passing of the spirit from this state of being to the next has often been observed by those possessing the clairvoyant faculty. I have known one whose clairvoyant power has been active on many occasions, and she has affirmed as a result of her experiences that there are no sudden deaths in the sense we think of them. She affirms that whenever anyone dies, there are in attendance certain spirits whose duty it is to help the soul in its passing, and these spirits are trained for this work.

Now I feel we do well to link up our experiences in this life with those in the higher realms. Many of the processes which we see in nature are regarded as automatic, but that does not rule out an inherent intelligence which guides them. When we reach the higher forms of life, we see the mothers careful about making some preparation for the new life about to emerge ; even the cuckoo sees to it that its young shall be cared for by some bird. Thus throughout nature, even among insects, we see a preparation for the new arrivals, and in many cases an effort to protect the young. The higher up the scale we go, the greater care do we see exercised; preparations become more elaborate, and when we reach the human kingdom, this preparation for the incoming life becomes the subject for much thought on the part of the parents.

Now death is a new birth ; can we then regard it as being a matter of less care and thoughtful provision than the birth of a child into this life ? If analogy holds, I do not think so. Wherever help is needed, there it is given, and while, to us, a passing may be sudden, it is apparently not so to those who watch over us. The signs of approaching dissolution, which may be imperceptible to us, are observed by those in the larger life ; and I have been assured by my clairvoyant friend that those in the next stage of existence are aware of any changes which may be near, although to us they might seem drastically sudden.

This does not mean that those who pass out are aware of the care and attention of those who minister to them. In that experience we shall probably be as unconscious as we are of being born, but that we shall be helped through it is, I think, only natural. I desire to put this clearly, for there seems some confusion in many minds about this. When the spirit is finally free from the flesh, his state and condition will be in accordance with his moral and spiritual development. He will, if his life has been evil, be in a self-created darkness, in which he will see only the reflections of his own nature. He may be so close to material things that he is unable to realize the change which has taken place, and may think he is still on earth; but these states are subsequent to the change, and do not affect the question of careful provision made for the reception of new life on the other side.

Perhaps the best description of a soul's passing is that given by Dr. Andrew Jackson Davis. I give it here, merely saying that the account has been confirmed by other observers. He says:*

When the hour of her death arrived, I was fortunately in a proper state of body and mind to induce the Superior Condition; but, previous to throwing my spirit into that condition, I sought the most convenient and favourable position, that I might be allowed to make the observations entirely unnoticed and undisturbed. . . . Thus situated and conditioned, I proceeded to observe and investigate the mysterious processes of dying, and learn what it is for an individual to undergo the change consequent upon physical death or external dissolution. They were these:

I saw that the physical organization could no longer subserve the diversified purposes or requirements of the Spiritual Principle. But the various internal organs of the body appeared to *resist* the withdrawal of the animating soul. . . . The body and the soul, like two friends, strongly resisted the various circumstances which rendered their eternal separation imperative and absolute. These internal conflicts gave rise to manifestations of what seemed to be, to the material senses, the most thrilling and painful sensations; but I was unspeakably thankful and delighted when I perceived and realized the fact that those physical manifestations were indications, *not of pain or unhappiness*, but simply that the spirit was eternally dissolving its co-partnership with the material organism.

Now the head of the body became suddenly enveloped in a fine,

*In *Light* of April 1935 appeared an account written by Dr. Riblet which corroborates the observations of Dr. A. J. Davis.

soft, mellow, luminous atmosphere ; and, as instantly, I saw the cerebrum and the cerebellum expand their most interior portions ; I saw them discontinue their appropriate galvanic functions ; and then I saw that they became highly charged with the vital electricity and vital magnetism which permeate subordinate systems and structures. That is to say, the brain, as a whole, suddenly declared itself to be tenfold more positive, over the lesser portions of the body, than it ever was during the period of health. This phenomenon invariably precedes physical dissolution.

Now the process of dying, or of the spirit's departure from the body, was fully commenced. The brain began to attract the elements of electricity, magnetism, of motion, of life, of sensation, into its various and numerous departments. The head became intensely brilliant ; and I particularly remarked that just in the same proportion as the extremities of the organism grew dark and cold, the brain appeared light and glowing.

Now I saw, in the mellow, spiritual atmosphere, which emanated from and encircled the head, the indistinct outlines of the *formation* of another head ! . . . This new head unfolded more and more distinctly ; and so indescribably compact and intensely brilliant did it become that I could neither see through it nor gaze upon it as steadily as I desired. While this spiritual head was being eliminated and organized from out of, and above, the material head, I saw that the surrounding aromal atmosphere which had emanated from the material head was in great commotion ; but, as the new head became more distinct and perfect, this brilliant atmosphere disappeared.

With inexpressible wonder, and with a heavenly and unutterable reverence, I gazed upon the holy and harmonious processes that were going on before me. In the identical manner in which the spiritual head was eliminated and unchangeably organized, I saw, unfolding in their natural, progressive order, the harmonious development of the neck, the shoulders, the breast, and the entire spiritual organization. It appeared from this, even to an unequivocal demonstration, that the innumerable particles of what might be termed unparticled matter, which constitute man's spiritual principle, are constitutionally endowed with certain elective affinities, analogous to an immortal friendship. The innate tendencies, which the elements and essences of her soul manifested by uniting and organizing themselves, were the efficient and imminent causes which unfolded and perfected her spiritual organization. The defects and deformities of her physical body were, in the spiritual body which I saw thus developed, almost completely removed. In other words, it seemed that those hereditary obstructions and influences were now removed, which originally arrested the full and proper development of her physical constitution; and, therefore, that her spiritual constitution, being elevated above those obstructions, was enabled to unfold and perfect itself, in accordance with the universal tendencies of all created things.

While this spiritual formation was going on, which was perfectly visible to my spiritual perceptions, the material body manifested, to the outer vision of observing individuals in the room, many symptoms of uneasiness and pain; but these indications were totally deceptive; they were wholly caused by the vital or spiritual forces drawn from the extremities and viscera into her brain, and thence into the ascending organism.

The spirit rose at right angles over the head or brain of the deserted body. But immediately previous to the final dissolution of the relationship which had for so many years subsisted between the spiritual and material bodies, I saw—playing energetically between the feet of the elevated spiritual body and the head of the prostrate physical body—a bright stream or current of vital electricity.

This taught me that what is customarily termed *Death* is but a *Birth* of the spirit from a lower into a higher state; that an inferior body and mode of existence are exchanged for a superior body of corresponding endowments and capabilities of happiness. I learned that the correspondence between the birth of a child into this world, and the birth of the spirit from the material body into a higher world, is absolute and complete—even to the *umbilical cord*, which was represented by the thread of vital electricity, which, for a few minutes, subsisted between and connected the two organisms together. And here I perceived, what I had never before obtained a knowledge of, that a small portion of this vital electrical element returned to the deserted body, immediately subsequent to the separation of the umbilical thread; and that this portion of this element which passed back

into the earthly organism instantly diffused itself through the entire structure, and thus prevented immediate decomposition.

From this account we see how unreasonable excessive grief can be. In the passing of any soul, our attitude should be one of calm trust. Indeed, much of our grief is selfish, for we are thinking of our loss, and not of the gain of the one who passes on. An unselfish love would rejoice in the liberation which death gives, and instead of repining and endeavouring in its possessiveness to draw the loved one back, would, in spirit, go out to help it through the change.

Regarding the removal of the body, this should not take place until there are definite signs that the spirit has left it. In temperate climes, three days should elapse before burial or cremation. Once the spirit is free of the body, there is no shock in this latter method of disposing of it ; besides, it is more healthful than burial, which, after all, has in it an element of materialism. One can understand those who believe in the resurrection of the body wishing it to be preserved, but for those who know what death is, cremation is more rational.

It is comforting to note that the usual signs of mourning are passing away. More rational views of death are spreading amongst the people, and, with a truer understanding of it, we realize that it is not a time for grief, but for quiet joy over the release of our friends from the narrow confines of the flesh. Let us do all things "decently and in order", without show and unnecessary ceremony. We can respect, honour, and revere the memory of our beloved without pomp, for that can only express some semblance of what we feel. Rest assured our true feelings will be known to those who have gone hence ; they will have neither part nor lot in the display we make over their bodies. The serene assurance that all is well with them is all they need, and all that is necessary for us to reveal to our friends on earth. Lavish funerals are often nothing but a display of pride and selfishness. With clearer light this sort of thing will pass away, and simplicity with dignity will be the prevailing note in our funerals.

The Reality of the Spirit-life

All that has been said implies that the next stage of existence is one that is as real as our own. Indeed, our friends on the other side insist that it is more real, that for them life is intensely vivid, with an aliveness which we cannot conceive. They insist that their life is one of human interests, full of the joy of service. It is perfectly organized, for it is based upon the law of rhythm ; each to his affinities and state, there to develop those capacities essential to further growth.

Let us reason a moment. What is the purpose of work ? One of the things we resent is the compulsion which circumstances impose upon us to perform uncongenial tasks. If we accept the view that whatever happens is in accordance with law, we shall not be so puzzled as we often are ; we shall, if we are honest, realize that the things from which we suffer, or those which we resent, originate in us. *We meet our mental states in the changing circumstances of our lives.*

Now work, rightly understood, is a means whereby we express our creativeness. It may be urged that much of the work in the world, such as minding machines, does not afford people any means of expressing their creative powers. True though this is, it does not affect the fundamental purpose of work. Power does not lie in environment alone, it lies rather in the *attitude we adopt towards it.* Therefore, I regard work not as a means to keep body and soul together, but as a means whereby the real man should find expression. Although some profess a dislike for work, you will often find them pursuing some hobby with ardent zeal. Even the man who works at hard manual labour will often at the end of the day work equally hard in his garden. This he calls recreation, not work; yet it is more truly work than the tasks he has been doing during the day; it is the time when he re-creates and gives expression to his love of nature.

This creativeness of the spirit may express itself either through manual or mental toil. Many live in their hands, some in their heads—I leave it to your imagination in what other parts of their bodies some people dwell. Those who express themselves through their hands require substances to mould and fashion, while those who express themselves mentally mould the plastic substances of the mental world and give us literature, and the fine arts, which demand a combination of hand and brain.

This has a definite bearing upon the reality of the spirit-world. Correspondingly we shall expect that in the early stages of spirit-life everything will be adapted to the needs of those who dwell there. In the many accounts which have come through, we are informed of the wondrous buildings, their furnishings, together with park-lands and many other features which make the early stages of the next life an idealized earth. What then will people do in that state? How are houses and temples created? How are gardens laid out? How does the scientist carry out his researches? Does he need apparatus for his experiments? Does the artist require canvas and pigments? The sculptor, wood, stone, or metal? For, although it may be argued that these things may be shaped by thought, there must be *substance* that is so shaped. Even here we construct in our minds, we see mentally that which we desire to construct, and on its own plane the mental conception is real.

Now the next stage of life will be as this in one respect—it will be both subjective and objective; existence demands this. Also, its environment will be as the natural environment of this plane. True it may be, and possibly is, more responsive to our wills than is our environment here; but think of the confusion if there were no stability! Suppose everyone's outer world were different from every other? We each of us here have our own inner world, but our environment is stable. We do not disagree about hills, valleys, rivers, lakes, seas, heat, cold, and the natural phenomena of this state. Is it not logical to assume that a like stability obtains in the next state of life? We may live a more vivid subjective life, and we may even, in some degree, share it with others; but when living objectively, a tree, a building, or fine scenery will be seen alike by all, with just those differences of perception that we find amongst people here.

Now apply this, and we see the purpose of work.

In the early stages of the next life each will find the tasks, whatever they may be, best suited to educing his creative ability. If through the hand, there will be workshops; if through science, laboratories; if through literature, libraries ; if through teaching, the lecture room. Everything will be provided to help each to give of his best and at the same time develop his own powers.

Through labour we shall learn to co-ordinate our powers. By experiment we shall discover how, by the power of our will, we can produce changes in substances. We shall get an inside view of life ; we shall be able to transfer our consciousness to the flora and fauna of that state and learn from within the many processes of life going on. From this to the practical application of such knowledge will be but a step, and we shall learn how to initiate the life process. how to guide and direct it, and by experiment develop our powers so that we may intelligently co-operate with the inherent consciousness ot the cosmos. This view, I am sure, makes the next stage of life one that is rational, and in line with what we know of the natural processes of the world.

I do not wish it to be thought that the next life is all beauty. Beauty is in the eye of the beholder. We should hardly expect the mean, grasping, avaricious, and evil-minded folks to dwell amid scenes of beauty. They also create in accordance with their inner states. If the mind be evil, filled with meanness and selfish ambitions, what can be the natural expression ? Hardly one of loveliness. "The kingdom of heaven is within you." So is the kingdom of hell, if we create it. In the end we shall find that we are the masters or the servants of a destiny which we ourselves create.

Spirit Intercourse and Spirit Communion

And now a word on the intercommunion of the two states oi existence. At the risk of being repetitive I must emphasize the need of lifting our minds above the state of mere conversation with our arisen friends. Everyone who has once proven the fact of survival should be content with that proof, and instead of constantly seeking to converse with his friends, strive for something beyond it.

Now I know from personal experience the intense joy which such communion can give, but it should not be regarded, as it so often is, as an end, but as a means to richer life. After all, much that we here call love is a pale semblance of the reality. Often it has too much self in it; it seeks to hold, to enslave; it is too possessive, and is rarely ready to give up anything the one beloved may gain. Has it ever occurred to you that we may injure by a too excessive love? Real love "suffereth long, and is kind; envieth not, is not puffed up, seeketh not its own", but ever strives to enrich the lives of others. How can one express this? God has clothed Himself with the universe as a mantle, and constantly pours His own love—life—through it. He serves in every part. He shares His love with all.

Now it is possible that we may through a lesser love come to a realization of this greater love, come to see in the Beloved the manifestation of the Father, and through it come to an understanding of the supreme and only Love, the love which we should have for God.

The only way we can manifest this is by loving one another; therefore in our desire to commune with our friends on the other side let us see to it that we do not hinder their progress by an excessive possessiveness. We share one life, one love, one being, and in that sharing must ever be ready to give all, that the whole may be enriched. Beyond spirit intercourse lies that state where we may experience spiritual communion, and this does not require any medium or séance room. It can be experienced at any time and in any place. One might walk the dull prosaic streets of a city, and yet be in heaven. If the soul is aspiring and the whole man alive in God, then for that soul death does not exist, for he dwells for ever in the light.

CHAPTER II

AN OUTLINE OF THE PHILOSOPHY OF SPIRITUALISM

The Term Spiritualism—Man and the Universe—Good and Evil—Determinism or Free Will ?—What is our Destiny ?

The Term Spiritualism

Spiritualism is the doctrine that all is spirit, or idealism. Behind the phenomena of the universe is One Reality. All that exists is an expression of it, form being its presentation in time. This Reality, religion calls God, who is Spirit, and whom we are told we must "worship in spirit and in truth". The word Spiritualism implies the reality of God, and it is against the background of Divine Reality that we must view the external universe.

Actually there are only two philosophies : Spiritualism and Materialism. Although Spiritualism does not deny the value of matter as a means of expression, Materialism does not acknowledge spirit as a reality. Today, mechanistic ideas of the universe are being superseded. It is now being realized that to think of the universe as a machine implies mechanical principles, and this, in turn, a mind that thinks in terms of mechanics. To make life dependent upon the machine for its origin is putting the cart before the horse. Analogy proves that before a machine can be constructed you must have a mind which can formulate the principles of mechanics and apply them. Ruling God out of the universe is like looking at an engine to find the engineer who constructed it. A self-created, self-directing, and self-governing machine is a contradiction, for creation, direction, and government imply mind, not mechanism.

The difficulty has been felt by many philosophers and scientists; even Haeckel found that when he ruled God out of the universe he had to introduce Him under another name. God is a necessary postulate; Infinite Self must be precedent to finite selves. God is.

Man and the Universe

It is curious how the obvious is overlooked. Men will argue about the origin of this, that, and the other, will gaily rule out any explanation which demands recognition of a Divine Being, and glibly speak of consciousness as an epiphenomenon, declaring that when man dies he ceases to be. Consciousness, they say, is a function of the brain, yet it is consciousness which questions and enables them to deny its persistence, even to affirm it has no real existence! When we press as to the purpose of the universe, we are told it has none; how can they think so when they believe we are but ephemeral beings who dance and sing, suffer and die? Those who believe this can only regard the universe as a gigantic mistake, a blind, unreasoning machine grinding out life to no purpose. Could nescience go further? Could there be a more dreary, arid, and barren view of life than this?

Reasonable as is the view that the universe is purposive, it would be a conceit for us to affirm that we know precisely what is the purpose, or purposes, of its existence. One view is that material existence is essential to the development and unfoldment of individuality. There is something more, for individuality unfolds character, and character is destiny. The purpose of earthly life is to bring out the latent qualities of the spirit, so that we may be prepared and equipped for the fuller life beyond. It is, therefore, of great importance that we strive to discover for ourselves the best means for developing the hidden powers of our being.

In viewing the universe, we see those aspects of it which are more or less in accord with our mental and spiritual development. One stresses the beauty of life, another its pain and suffering. We should strive to see life whole, and not concentrate upon one or two aspects of it. Optimism and pessimism are simply different sides of the same shield ; actually life is a blend, there being no sharp divisions as systems of thought imply. To see life whole we must look at it as we would a picture, and we shall then see that light and shade are essential, are complementary. Naturally, we are disposed to look at the universe from the personal rather than from the universal point of view and, so doing, see in it the reflections of our selves. It requires some effort to set self on one side and step outside the personal and regard oneself, with all else, against the background of Eternal Becoming.

If we transcend the personal, we discover the larger self who holds in balance all opposites, and unites the diversities of life in a coherent harmony. *It is not what we demand from the universe, but what we are prepared to give to it that is the measure of our spiritual development.* One may seek to escape the ills of life, or one may use them to achieve the attainment of the Christ Ideal. The ideas of escape and attainment are the great difference between

East and West. Both demand abandonment to the ideal, but the motives are different ; for one seeks escape from self by the annihilation of self, the other seeks the realization of the greater Self through the vicissitudes of life. One overcomes by indifference, the other by intensity of living. The method we use depends upon the degree of clearness of our inner light.

Good and Evil

The development and practice of mediumship increases the responsibilities of the sensitive who exercises these powers. Like his fellows, he sees the many difficulties with which the path of life is strewn and, if he reflects upon his mediumship at all, cannot but question what bearing, if any, his mediumship has upon the vivid contrasts which life presents. The increased sensitivity which the unfoldment of mediumistic powers brings is not an unmixed blessing, and the medium will be as earnest in his search to uncover the underlying principles of life as the most eager of philosophers. He will seek, as others have done, to unravel the mystery of good and evil.

Religion affirms that God is Love, and immediately man asks: "Would a God of Love countenance the many evils which we see in the world ?" The answer to this depends upon our conception of love. The tendency is to regard love in a sentimental rather than in a reasonable sense. Feeling that we wish to aid and protect those we love, we often do our utmost to shield them from danger, and when they happen to go wrong, or evince some degree of independence of thought, expressing views with which we do not agree, we are distressed. True love is not possessive; much that passes for love is disguised selfishness, and we need to be watchful that our affections do not inveigle us into imagining we are doing right, when we are seeking, not the welfare of the beloved, but our own personal comfort and peace of mind.

In speaking of the love of God we usually have in view *our* ideas of love, and in our earnestness we clothe God with our own attributes, thinking that if we would not do such-and-such, God would not. We must strive to realize that the love of God is far above that of man, and instead of blaming God for the evils in the world, or denying them as some do, let us ask what is their purpose.

Good and evil are relative to our development. They are contrasts, and outside of consciousness do not exist. It is through our unfolding consciousness that we see such contrasts. Even in our life we find things change, and, relatively speaking, the good of today becomes the evil of tomorrow. Evil is a problem set for our solution. Let us take natural phenomena such as storms, earthquakes, etc.—things over which, at present, we have no control. If there were no conscious beings in the world, such questions as the good or evil of these phenomena would not arise. As they are part of the order of the world, man does not sit down and conclude that nothing can be done to combat them. He accepts the challenge and applies his mind to minimizing their effects. So successful has he been, that today there is a greater margin of safety than there was a few years ago. By and by, as he grows, he will obtain control of these natural forces, and what today are regarded as evils will gradually cease to exist.

The same applies to the ills which afflict the body. Diseases are problems we have to solve. One of the reasons for our existence upon this plane is to gain a knowledge of how to control our bodies. A fuller understanding of mediumship will ultimately lead to this, and we shall find that those powers which today seem to be abnormal will, by and by, be seen to be a means by which we may gain a more complete knowledge of the inner mechanism of the body, together with a mastery of it.

The pessimist croaks: "Why did not God create a perfect world?" Well, he has created a perfect world. The pessimist's view of perfection is static, not dynamic; it is finality and boredom, not full of interest and becoming. The pessimist's cry when pushed to its logical conclusion is borne of laziness; he desires to look and understand without effort. It may be his idea of perfection, but to me it looks suspiciously like hell; for one would be consumed with ennui.

Man accepts the challenge of disease, though perhaps not always wisely, but he meets it and acts according to his knowledge and development. A few years ago, he marched in processions to his church with candles burning, singing psalms, and offering prayers to God for him to intercede and stay the plague. Further back. he offered sacrifices of beasts, birds, and before that even human beings. It is, however, questionable whether we have advanced so far beyond this primitive stage as appearances would have us believe. When one remembers the horrors that go on in the name of scientific research, it would seem that we are still in the age of ignorance, the difference being that the so-called scientist has usurped the functions of the priest. However, where common sense has sway and we conform to the suggestions of the sanitary engineer, disease gives way to health. One of man's greatest enemies is dirt, whether it be in rubbish dumps or poured into a pure blood-stream in the form of serums. We might well establish an old goddess, Hygeia, and worship her in a common-sense way.

But, someone will say, look at the pain and suffering involved, is it not an awful price to pay? Yes, the price is heavy, but we value our gains in proportion to the effort we make to get them. Pain is the natural law of protection. The nerves through which we feel pain are the same as those which thrill with pleasure. To illustrate: If we felt no pain and accidentally put our hand into the fire, it would be consumed without our being aware of it. When the X-rays were discovered, man had no knowledge that undue exposure to them was injurious. *He felt no pain,* and it was only by sad experiment that their danger became known. As the rays are not commonly met with, nature has had no need to develop a sense to warn us of their danger. We feel no pain in their presence and so are not protected. Pain is a signal that something is wrong, and as long as there is life in the body, the possibility of pain as well as pleasure is there too. By and by, when we have learned to use our bodies wisely, pain will be rare, and we can look forward to its ceasing to be a necessary experience.

There is another function which is apt to be overlooked: pain is a great awakener of sympathy. Before we can truly sympathize with another we must at some time have experienced a similar condition to theirs. Pain does bind us together; it is often the handmaiden of love; it *opens our eyes,* promoting feelings of sympathy from which love is born. It gives understanding. When the ancient scribe spoke of the Messiah as a "man of sorrows and acquainted with grief", he illustrated the profound truth that the root of God's love is in pain. God immanent in humanity suffers and rejoices in humanity. All that humanity experiences of pain and suffering, or joy and gladness, God does also.

When we turn to the moral aspect of the problem, men ask: "Why are some men evil ?" If we view this problem in the manner suggested by the foregoing, we shall see that the difference between a good and an evil man is one of development. No man seeks evil, all seek good. Get to the root of it and you will see that it is so. The man who loves a life of self-seeking pleasure is not seeking evil. He is looking for good, selfishly perhaps, but he is not thinking of evil. I suppose that the majority of us want a good time, and it is not evil to wish so ; the evil arises in our manner of seeking to satisfy that natural craving. When a man robs another he is thinking of *the good* the proceeds of the robbery will bring to himself. Whatever prevents us from experiencing largeness of life we count as evil. More life is what we seek. When we seek wrongly and cause suffering to others, we in turn suffer ; and here again we see the function of pain. "Though I make my bed in hell, Thou art there", sang the Psalmist. Yes, God is there, in the form of pain, to turn the wanderer home.

Determinism or Free Will ?

Man, says the determinist, is the product of heredity and environment. His conception of law is so rigid that he seeks to apply it to every department of life.

In discussing the problem of good and evil, we find that in the moral world the question of man's freedom is of great importance. With it is bound up the question of moral responsibility. The rigid determinist reduces his philosophy to an absurdity—it has been aptly termed the "can't-help-it philosophy". Determinism is influenced by the mechanistic views of nature which modern science is giving up.

In the inorganic kingdom we can trace the operation of law with some degree of certitude. An astronomer can predict the motions of a planet, but a biologist cannot predict the motions of a fly ! When we reach the kingdom of life, we find there a spontaneity and freedom that is absent from the inorganic kingdom. If we say that organisms obey the urge of life, it is because they are life. As we rise from instinct to reason, we find the freedom of the individual forms of life increases. The power of selection becomes increasingly wider, until, when we reach the human kingdom, the sense of freedom is common to all. We *feel* free, every one of us, and if we are compelled to do things we are not willing to do, we do them with a resentment that indicates that our freedom has been outraged. This sense of freedom is so precious that we are ready to fight for it, endure torture, and go to the stake for it. One cannot regard it as an illusion. It is not so much in the material world as in the world of mind that we enjoy freedom. "Stone walls do not a prison make, nor iron bars a cage", and we all feel this to be true.

Heredity is the sum of all those ancestral influences which are expressed in our bodies. That this has an influence on our mental life no one will deny, but it is a mistake to regard it as the final authority, even in combination with environment. The determinist does not deny that man has choice. What he argues is that it is determined for him by his heredity and environment, that man can only choose in accordance with these influences. But it is not heredity or environment which decides. *We do the deciding,* and that is where our freedom of choice comes in. Who is this we or I ? The body ? No, it is something which uses the body, therefore we *use* our heredity and environment to determine our choice.

That is the difference between the determinist and the believer in rational free will. It is certain there can be no morality without a sense of personal responsibility. A man is either free or not free to do a certain thing. The truth in determinism is destroyed when it is applied without discrimination. Our sense of freedom and of moral responsibility is a growing one As we develop, so does our freedom increase; we gradually acquire the power to use the law instead of allowing the law to use us.

Our conceptions are at fault, for there can be no true freedom without law. The believer in free will sometimes speaks as if law was of no account, though he does not hesitate to use law to punish those who do wrong. Law is one side of the shield and freedom the other. Without law you have chaos, and that is not freedom. Freedom for development demands law, so that it may proceed in an orderly manner. Think what our social life would be if, in the interests of freedom, we abandoned law and order. Our civilization would become an even worse scramble than it is at present. The problem we have to solve is to have the effectiveness of instinct united to the freedom of reason. The logic of determinism is seen in the hive-bees and the ants, in which the individual is sacrificed to the whole ; he is a mere cog in the machine, has no freedom of choice, living by the inherent urge of his instinctive impulses. No one wishes to see that translated into the human world, though a rational application of it could, with advantage, be made to many of our problems.

The value of personality is so tremendous, that nature has striven for milleniums to produce it in its fullest form in man. The fine flower of personality is seen in Jesus. The transcendent value of it is such that the very thought of annihilation is abhorrent, even to those who believe it is the end of man. If they accept this view it is none the less a tragedy to them. For its fullest development, personality demands the power, and claims it as a right, to be free to choose its path, and in so doing makes clear its sense of moral responsibility.

Descartes said: "I think, therefore I am." I will reverse it: "I am, therefore I think", for being is precedent to thinking. Thinking is a phenomenon of our being; it is the power by which we are enabled to govern and control our life. When we realize that, we are on the road to gain real freedom ; we know that even law will expand with our understanding of it. If we reflect upon the powers of mediumship, of what some through special training can do. can we sit down and regard ourselves as the slaves of law? No, we are to become the masters of law. Without freedom to experiment, to seek, to discover, we cannot attain the heights reached by the great souls of the race.

WHAT IS OUR DESTINY?

We have in some degree hinted at this. "Ye shall be as gods", said one of old—but we must not hurry to our conclusion. Let us glance back.

The history of humanity has been one of struggle and effort, of a long and patient march out of the mists of time into the clearer day of the present. Through suffering, trial, defeat, triumph, the spirit of man has gone on undaunted. Millions have fallen by the way, but the race goes on. In countless hearts have bloomed the fine ideals of self-sacrifice and loving service. Time after time man has laid down his life for what he has held to be true. His instinctive freedom has demanded the right to express what he has believed. Mistakes he has made, many and often, but we are catching a gleam of the peaks of realization, far off, and the reflection of the sun glinting on them inspires us with new and glorious vision. The ideal beckons us onward to further effort and more glorious service. Pray God that we be worthy, and true to the divine light within our souls.

Now we may confine our attention to this life alone, and one can only praise those who, believing death is the end, yet work for the amelioration of human suffering. Winwood Reade, in his *Martyrdom of Man*, proclaims his faith in the fine destiny of the race, but he says that belief in personal immortality must first be given up. Glorious as is his ideal of man going out to colonize the stars, and of our race spreading through the universe, it is, after all, that the universe may become a charnel house.

But we have an even more glorious vision. Knowing that man survives the change of death, we look beyond for the great realization of a destiny greater even than colonizing the stars! It is not decreed that we shall be confined to the worlds of matter—the realms of spirit invite our investigation, our efforts to solve the mystery of being. From stage to stage we shall rise. The ancient prophecy will be fulfilled: we "shall be as gods". Through the labour of hand and brain, through an ever widening knowledge of the finer forces of life, we shall learn how to control and direct them. We shall become creators, "imitators of God", as Paul puts it. All the fine promise which our nature holds will be fulfilled. Even now we see, in the growing expansion of consciousness which the development of our supernormal powers reveals, an exercise of those finer powers, indicating what is within our reach.

If I might assume the role of the prophet, I believe that in the new age we have entered we shall witness the mastery of mind over matter. For not only are we to become masters upon the inner realms, but masters of the outer courts of the Temples of Being. The powers of the spirit pouring into the world today are quickening the mind of the race. A new sense is stirring, and one great factor in this is the movement of Spiritualism, God-inspired and directed as I believe it is.

CHAPTER III

BEING

Self-Existence—Who or What is the Self?—Attributes of the Self—Rational Living.

SELF-EXISTENCE

REALITY is both subjective and objective. The objective world affects our senses, and in varying ways produces those stimuli which result in our conception of the world and the universe. But mediumship reveals that there are other aspects of life besides that of the purely material and physical conditions of which we are normally aware. What to the onlooker may seem to be purely subjective may, to the medium, be as objective as anything pertaining to our normal existence. There are worlds within worlds, and as we progress and become conscious of them, so do we find the boundaries of objective existence become larger. Mediumship means an expansion of being.

Self-existence is synonymous with self-consciousness. If we could cease to be, all else would, for us, also cease to be. Yet if a man is dead to this world, it still exists; hence it is a mistaken view which makes objective realities dependent upon our existence. The whole does not cease to exist because a part of it changes. The world existed long before life, as we know it, manifested; if it had not existed, we could not have any conception of it. The existence of the world is a necessary prelude to our advent upon it.

It is questionable whether we are right in denying consciousness to the world. "At the beginning of evolution," writes Gustave Geley in his work, *From the Unconscious to the Conscious*, "as far as we may be able to conceive such beginning, there is neither consciousness nor individualization." I think that this can only be so as regards material expression. Infinite self-consciousness is a necessary precedent to all unfoldment in form. While it may be true that self-consciousness as we know it is the result of evolutionary development, the germ of it always has been. It is not a derivative of something else, it is of the original Infinite Self. If it be argued that there cannot be an Infinite Self, that original consciousness is impersonal, whence come Self and Personality if they do not originate from Infinite Being?

To put it in terms of religion: we are because God is; and we experience and express self-hood because God is the supreme Self. We are the Infinite in expression. We should remember this when we use such terms as unconscious and conscious, impersonal and personal; they are verbal conveniences which deal with certain aspects of Being. In the Infinite all paradoxes find their solution, all opposites meet at the centre. For us that centre is our own Self. We are.

Who or What is the Self?

The study of mediumship enlarges our conceptions of personality and self-hood. What is that blending of personality that takes place in spirit-control? The submergence of one personality and the emergence of another, with entirely different reactions and memories to that of the sensitive, is a phenomenon of profound interest to the student. The simple explanation that the medium is used to express the thoughts, mannerisms, and personality of another being whom the world regards as dead is not really so simple as it seems to be; it leaves much to our imaginations. Personality presents so many problems, is so many-sided, and sometimes so contradictory as almost to seem to constitute different personalities.

Dissociation of personality is a well-known though little understood phenomenon. There are various opinions as to whether the self is a unity or a combination of mental states. If we accept the premise of an Infinite Self, the unity of That Self will be seen, not as a combination of many aspects, but as One Self manifesting in an infinite variety of ways; thus, although we have all opposites, they are unified in the One Self. If we apply this reasoning to the lesser selves, we shall see that each has a centre of unity which preserves its individuality.

In mediumship, then, there is a blending of personalities but not a superseding of the medium's original self. That co-operates with another for a specific object. This indicates—to use a humorous expression—that mediums are not all there! There is a significance in this phrase quite other than the humour of it would lead one to believe, for it suggests that in many respects a medium's activities are not confined to this realm; that he may, without any awareness of his normal consciousness, be active on other realms and carrying out important work in them. As the Infinite Self manifests as many, so in lesser degree does that of man when he reaches that stage of growth where his psychic faculties can become active.

Every aspect of life is personal in the original sense of that word, form being a mask through which the Original Self manifests. In the lower degrees of life there is no sense of individuality, no awareness of "I", but as we ascend the tree of life we find its branches expressing a more definite individuality, until we reach complete self-consciousness.

It is well to keep in mind the difference between individuality and personality ; the latter is a manifestation of the former. One might say that personality is *individuality in action.* Personality both hides and reveals ; there are times when the real "Me" peeps out ; there are others when it is hidden. Our bodies are masks, and behind them are all kinds of loyalties and deceits. The capacity for good or evil is in the self, and according to its development will be its manifestation of either.

Who are we ? The phenomena of mediumship hints at mysterious depths, especially when we experience alternations of personality. Are the dissociations so well known to the psychologist out manifestations or facets of the One Self? Some cases of dissociation seem to indicate a psychical invasion, the imposition of another personality, similar to the phenomenon of spirit-control. Cases are not unknown where the manifesting personality has declared that it was a spirit. Obsession is not unknown, and such an authority as Dr. Hyslop said, as stated previously, that he fought against the idea of obsession for ten years, but had to admit the fact in the end. We will remember that Doctors Wickland and Bull both spend their lives dealing with cases of obsession, and they affirm that many cases of lunacy are obsessions. Other doctors have come to similar conclusions.

Bearing this in mind, we shall see that the problem of one or many selves is bound up with this phenomenon. The question, Who is the self? may, in this respect, mean that the self temporarily manifesting is a spirit who, through ignorance or perhaps eagerness to manifest its presence, has become entangled in the aura of some psychically susceptible person, the distortion of ideas being due to lack of proper control by the spirit. Such people are not mad, they are simply manifesting an incipient mediumship.

In hypnotic experiment we know a subject will manifest in an appropriate manner any personality suggested to him. We do not say because of this that the subject is many personalities, any more than an actor who takes many parts is many persons. The centralizing factor in all these manifestations is the self, which adapts itself to express the dominant idea. There must be some centre of stability from which the phenomenon starts, and which is able to control the various expressions. It will be noted that in all such manifestations there is something of the original self. We find this in spirit-control; no matter how complete it is, or however vividly the spirit is able to reveal himself, there is always something which cannot be entirely suppressed or transcended. Even in some forms of materialization, the first manifestations are like the medium. All this emphasizes the strength of the real Self; it is original, distinctive, yet sufficiently pliable to lend itself to many forms of expression.

The Self is the original power behind all forms of expression, the unifying factor at the heart of All Being, the source of all that is. It is transcendent and immanent;

it is above form, but lives in form. It is the unity which manifests in the trinity of life, consciousness, and substance.

Regarding obsession, I would here emphasize that the best safeguard against it is the rational development of one's mediumistic powers. In these cases the victim can do more than any other to help himself. He must exercise his will and be master in his own house.

Attributes of the Self

The outstanding characteristic of man is his power to reason. Unlike other forms of life he is not entirely under the sway of instinct, revealing an ability to adapt himself to changing circumstances far beyond that of other creatures. It has been said that man is born with a note of interrogation in his brain, and certainly his ability to ask and answer questions exceeds that of any other animal. His life shows a constant effort to advance. Often reason opposes instinct, and then he is subject to unrest and turmoil, until one or the other conquers, or there is a solution of the problem which satisfies both sides of his being.

Present-day psychology stresses the influence of the unconscious, which certainly exercises a great power upon our lives. It would seem that man is still struggling to bring this underworld of himself under the dominion of reason. There are worlds of difference between a being who is merely a bundle of reflexes swayed by the dominant influence of the moment and one whose life is directed by reason. The influences which at times swirl up from the unconscious can be devastating; and one of our principal duties is to gain control of this under-world, so that its primitive forces may be directed into channels which make for higher living.

One of the efforts of the medium should be to control this underworld of his being. Unless he does, he will find that his mediumship will lose much of its value and force, and he will become like a boat without compass or rudder. Self-control is as essential as spirit-control.

Although reason is such an outstanding characteristic of man, it must be admitted that the age of reason has hardly begun. Nations are still very much at the mercy of the primitive impulses in human nature. Few people really think, and in argument one notes how they run off at a tangent and get lost in side issues, which confuse and do not affect the principle under discussion. Politicians are masters of the art of side-tracking, and so confusing issues that at last the original theme of discussion is lost sight of.

Perhaps the most powerful influence in our nature is love. This, being an expression of our emotional nature, may be said to be instinctive. If it has its roots in sex, the branches of the tree are in heaven. Man reveals a power of sacrifice beyond anything in the rest of creation. Some of the higher animals come near him in this respect, but for long endeavour and persistent effort man is supreme. Ordinary relationships are transcended, and history is replete with examples which inspire us with feelings of the noblest and most unselfish kind. Allied to it is the power of persistence which carries man over all obstacles and difficulties. He never knows defeat—repulses, yes, but they only nerve him to greater effort. In these he often reveals a passion of self-sacrifice which lifts him to the level of divinity.

Intuition may be defined as instinct become self-conscious. We know very little about it, though we are aware of its power in our lives. By it we are able to arrive at conclusions with certitude, though we may find it difficult to give any reason for our conclusions. Reason likes to see the links in the chain; intuition leaps forward to its objective with such swiftness that reason is left breathless and often doubting. Those in whom this faculty is strong are more intuitive than logical. A combination of both is ideal, but rarely met with.

Reason, intuition, and persistence vary enormously in individuals, for each tends to express the norm of his development. If we could see a graph of our inner life, we should see it as a wavy line, with, I hope, a tendency to rise higher and higher. This would reveal another characteristic, that of progression, the tendency to self-improvement. The whole of history exemplifies this desire of life to express itself in an ever-expanding spiral of progressive unfoldment. Arbitrary divisions break down; life is no longer sharply divided into classes; the value of the individual increases, despite appearances to the contrary; the feeling of solidarity grows, and the great thing is to unite this with the progressive forces which preserve individuality. At the present time the dominance of the machine is apt to make for a standardization, which limits rather than provides what it should—greater opportunity for individual unfoldment.

Rational Living

Mediums should live rationally. That one can be used for the giving of spirit messages does not set one apart from the rest of one's fellows. Usually, mediums are very common-sense folk who take their mediumship in a rational manner. Our first duty is to self, neglect of which ends in a form of parasitism. In eagerness to serve others, it sometimes happens that one becomes neglectful of self, with results that are disastrous. While it is true that one of the purposes of our existence here is to help others, it is also true that we are here to help ourselves, and how can we do that if we neglect our bodies ? A rational care of what has been termed the "temple of the living God" is essential to our development. We have to develop self-control ; to be able to say yes or no with decision. One cannot lay down hard and fast rules, for we all differ, and what one thrives on will cause another to pine. Read a few books on dietetics and you will see that in such matters one's own judgment and common sense must be one's guide.

One of the things we are apt to forget is that life is eternal. We often express discontent at our progress. If we get our perspective right, and view life against the background of Infinite Being, we shall not be so disgruntled. We shall see that so long as we are honestly striving, that is all that matters. We may not be the first in the race, but that matters little, for the thing of importance is the fitness gained in the training for it. That stands us in good stead after the race is run. Life is not a matter of mere accomplishment, or completed tasks, but the striving for expression. We are apt to think too much in finalities, of completed efforts, of perfection achieved, instead of which we should always be looking for further horizons, regarding all things as relative to increasing purposes. If we do this, we shall have the only contentment worth having, the being content to strive. The glory of the race is in the running of it, not the crown of laurel given to the victor.

We should conserve our energies so that we have that reserve necessary to meet any crisis in our lives. If we consider our lives, we shall probably find there has been, perhaps still is, much waste effort. In many of our workshops psychologists are endeavouring to teach people to co-ordinate their powers, to eliminate useless movements, and to direct their minds so that more work can be accomplished with less effort. The same principle if applied all round would mean richer health, more abundant energy, and a better directed life. To live rationally is to live according to the laws of our being; to co-ordinate our forces so that we express ourselves harmoniously. We are prone to burden ourselves with many wants, and obedience to the call of pleasure can be as exhausting as hard and strenuous labour; more so in fact. Pleasure has its place, but it should be re-creative. Pure hedonism does not result in happiness, it ends in satiety, unrest, and dissatisfaction.

Life should be spacious, wide, and ample in its interests, full of the joy of striving, with opportunities for expressing the creativeness of the spirit. We should live in the present, with no undue fret about the past, or anxiety about the future. This may seem ideal, but when we examine any system of philosophy or religion, it resolves itself into living our lives according to our inner light.

CHAPTER IV

SPECULATIVE

Immortality—Pre-existence—Emergence or Re-incarnation.

IMMORTALITY

THE dream of immortality has constantly recurred to the minds of men. From the far past come echoes which still vibrate in the world. In that far time, before ever a temple was reared, men dreamed of a life beyond, and the primitive mind peering through the mists of death saw the shadows which peopled the world of spirits. There is that in man which laughs at death, fearful and terrible though it may seem. Deep down in the human heart is the hope that leaps beyond the grave to find its realization of a more perfect life, in a world fairer than our fondest dreams. "As long as the lips of love shall kiss the lips of death," said a great agnostic, "the dream of immortality will haunt the minds of men."

But is it a dream? Survival of death has passed from dream to reality. We know now that death does not touch the essential man, though it may destroy the garment he wears. That death does not touch man may well be regarded as a promise of immortality; but it is not a fulfilment of it. Indeed, if immortality be thought of as mere duration, it is conceivable we should not wish for it. There must be something more than mere existence, a special quality of life; perhaps that which Jesus called the "eternal", which He declared could only be realized when we "know God".

We are not without evidence of a kind even in our physical world. We know the foundations of the material universe are invisible. When the light of science is turned upon matter, it vanishes into the ether, and we are forced to postulate an original something—call it ether or spirit—out of which all has been evolved. This primal spirit is everlasting, always has been, always will be. "End and beginning are dreams", in spirit they do not exist. We may speak of the universe as ever-becoming, but that can relate only to the outer manifestation of the One Power who was before worlds, and who will be when worlds are no more.

Religion declares that, as the universe originates in the One Reality, man does also. It affirms that in us is a spark of the one flame, which may be fostered and made to glow with ever increasing radiance until our whole being is filled with divine light. Seer, prophet, sage, mystic, all proclaim the same ideas, and we lesser gifted souls have, at times, felt the stirrings of divine life in our hearts.

Mediumistic phenomena are only pointers. They come within the region of scientific investigation and, in so far as they give evidence of survival, go to strengthen the affirmations of faith. We see clearly that these manifestations cannot do more than prove that we pass through the gate of death to a fuller life. The fact that man survives the change of death implies that he existed before birth. An immortal being cannot have a beginning; man must be viewed against the background of

Pre-existence

It may be objected that the soul does not originate, and that is true as to substance, but is it so of its individualization? The materialist, as we know, regards the soul as the sum total of our bodily functioning. That we know is not true, because it survives the death of the body. Some say that the soul is created by God at birth. There is no scientific evidence for it, for we know the child is alive before birth. The objection to the theory of the special creation of souls is rather a moral than a scientific one. It makes God a respecter of persons, for He gives to one soul a body which is predisposed to evil, and to another a body predisposed to good. It may be argued that morality is a question of how the soul uses the body; but is not the body an index to the character of the man? As Emerson says in his essay on "Fate":

> When each comes forth from his mother's womb, the gate of gifts closes behind him. Let him value his hands and his feet, he has but one pair. So he has but one future, and that is already predetermined in his lobes, and described in that little fatty face, pig-eye, and squat form. All privilege and all the legislation of the world cannot meddle or help to make a poet or a prince of him.
>
> Jesus said: "When he looketh on her, he hath committed adultery." But he is an adulterer before he has yet looked on the woman. By the superfluity of animal, and the defect of thought in his constitution, who meets him, or who meets her, in the street, sees that they are ripe to be each other's victim.

This is an extreme view ; one can only point out that there are facts which show that religion has the power to transcend even the hereditary proclivities to evil in a man. We can accept the facts, but we must not sit down and say, "Kismet". Man is his own fate.

The doctrine of pre-existence supposes that we exist in some state prior to our coming on this scene. Some affirm that we have a choice of conditions, that we choose in accordance with the light we have. Some elect one state, some another. It does not entirely satisfy, and is open to the same objections as the former theory. We labour under the difficulty that we cannot, at present, know the degree of enlightenment which souls have before making their choice. There is no demonstrable evidence that one has lived an individual existence before incarnating ; we can only speculate about probabilities. If we accept any doctrine of immortality, one can agree that there is a pre-existent background, but any theory must be not only philosophically, but morally satisfying.

The evolutionary theory regards the soul as the product of evolution, just as is the body. The soul exists in God prior to its manifestation. The act of creation sets it on its journey, and the nascent self comes into being through the involutionary and evolutionary processes. The whole is designed to bring out and fix the latent individuality of the soul. We become men, and in this view, while in substance we always have *been*, as conscious individuals we have a beginning. Now it is a metaphysical axiom that "what has a beginning will have an end", and it would seem we gain individuality only to lose it at some time. We may persist as conscious individuals only at last to become absorbed in God. "The dewdrop slips into the shining sea", and many hold the view that this is what will happen. It is difficult to understand what can be the purpose of such long travail, if in the end we are to lose our individuality and sink into the sea of undifferentiated life. Such a view appears as barren as materialism.

Emergence or Re-incarnation

One feels the need of a view of life which makes effort worth while. To many, the fact of survival is all that is needed to establish in their minds the purposiveness of the universe. But we seek for something more completely satisfying. From a close study of mediumship there emerge some views which are helpful in our search.

The exquisite balance of worlds, and the orderly sequence of phenomena, indicate the existence of universal law. To the materialist this may simply be but uniformities of co-existence and sequence. Law is a mode of being. All forms of matter are reducible to gas, and the researches of scientists are towards the hypothesis that all forms of matter are but different expressions of one universal substance. If we postulate a universal substance, it must exist prior to manifestation of it as suns, planets, etc. The postulate is necessary, because we cannot conceive of something being made from nothing. As Spinoza says: "I understand Substance to be that which is in itself and is conceived through itself, the conception of which does not depend on the conception of another thing from which it may be formed." It is the primordial stuff from which worlds and systems are made.

Substance must have attributes and modes of manifestation, and these we are made aware of by the phenomena of the universe. Life and mind may be regarded as attributes of universal substance. Perhaps it would be truer to say that universal substance is living and mental. Life and mind being omnipresent are inherent in universal substance, as the principles of organization. Thus life, mind, and organism (or substance) are inseparable. It is the basis of any conception of immortality.

In its primal state, life and mind manifest equally throughout the infinite extent of universal substance. As the principles of organization guided by the inherent intelligence become operative, there emerge the various planes of psychic and physical being, ultimating in the material universe. This may be considered as the outward manifestation of Divine Substance, or God, which on its journey from the within to the without, organizes the various planes of being. It is the impulsion of the Divine Thought, which is creative. Every step is one of limitation, until it reaches the most restricted of all, material existence. Viewed mystically, this is the great sacrifice, the voluntary subjection of the divine to the bondage of matter. We may consider this as part of a great plan, and the refining and spiritualizing of the material universe the great work of the Cosmic Spirit. There is thus the antithesis, the positive and the negative, which are ever essential to all creative effort. This is the mystery of generation, symbolized by the serpent entwining the egg.

Throughout the universe we find its rhythm is based on the musical octave. This is a law inherent in the Divine Mind. The octave of being is expressed through the seven planes, each coarser in grade than the one preceding it. These planes interpenetrate, and progress consists in becoming more aware of them through the development of perception. This long process entails, what to limited human consciousness is an eternity. The infinite Divine Mind (substance) pervades all, and is the basic rhythm of the whole. The original movement of the Divine Mind may be said to have precipitated a film of slightly denser substance, forming the highest plane of which our consciousness can become aware. It is of this substance that man's spiritual body is organized, and ever between it and the Divine Mind is the constant reciprocal flow of energizing Intelligence and Will. Incarnate man cannot reach this high state of consciousness. Matter necessarily inhibits him ; he must win his way through by self-conscious effort. Upon this plane the Divine Will manifests as purity and power.

The next movement—speaking logically, as these movements are not sequential but co-existent—results in the formation of the next plane, which is that of direct cognition, or intuition. Here the self may be said to glimpse its first awareness of self. With it comes the striving of all the latent energies and powers of being which flow through the finite selves. It is still diffused, and the organization of this direct cognition can only come by hard experience.

Following this plane is the next, that of pure intelligence (perception). Here the mind is split up by the prism of intellect. The pure white light of the spirit is no longer unified, but its separate rays, radiating from the central point of being in the finite self, are distorted and lack balance. It is necessary that the self become conscious of the component parts of the pure white light of the spirit. The first three planes, therefore, correspond to the three higher aspects of mind as expressed in man.

The fourth plane symbolizes the Christ principle, the unifier, midway between the higher and the lower aspects of the Divine Mind ; for every plane is an aspect of that Mind. Christ is the harmonizing principle, the power which lifts the lower creation by pouring out its life in service to all. It is the great spending power of the soul, whose far-flung radiance bathes all planes in heavenly light, mellowing, transmuting, and elevating the lower mind ; purifying and strengthening all qualities, infusing into them the courage to abandon self completely. It is the plane where the Divine and the Human meet, where the Father (God) and the Son (Humanity) reciprocally love and enjoy. It is the plane of immense energy, its dynamism energizing all lower planes. Its symbol is the Divine Man, standing with extended arms against the background of Heaven, expressive of complete abandon and perfect balance. "Before the world was, I was."

The fifth plane is that of desire, or emotion, where power flows outwards and downwards. The great work to be completed on this plane is the harmonizing and unifying of apparently conflicting desires. It is the root of action, but its limited outlook causes it to hold to itself. Self-preservation, self-aggrandisement, self-perpetuation —these are its incentives to action. It is here that evil arises, for desire is blind and wild, and must be tamed and made to see. It is the goad, the whip, the spur to effort. Wherever there is desire, there is action. Who is without desire ? Not the eradication, but the right direction of desire is the goal, and this can only be gained through sacrifice.

The sixth plane in the expression of life is the etheric aspect of Substance. It is the mould of the material, in fact is part of the physical universe. Ether permeates all matter, embodying the physiological principle of the Divine Mind; it provides the function which precedes organism. Through the etheric the Divine Idea becomes clothed in concrete form; the plane of matter is reached. This is the turning-point of the half-circle of Being—from the Divine Mind, through the various planes to the dense material, where, enriched with many experiences, the stream of finite selves goes back through the different planes to God, thus completing the circuit of Becoming.

This indicates that as life flows downwards it gathers experience on every plane, but we may regard it as life turned inward upon itself. It gathers from every plane what is essential to its completion. Each germ-self takes an atom from each plane, which becomes its point of contact with, and power to express itself upon, whatever plane the atom belongs to.

The ego may be said to be composed of groups of atoms pertaining to every expression of the Divine Mind on the various planes of Being. The ego has seven permanent atoms. These are latent, but eventually, through experience, the ego learns how to control and direct its energies through them, and also how to respond to the vibrations of the planes to which the respective atoms belong. Thus when the material plane is reached, life is first associated, through the permanent physical atom, with the mineral. The ego, through its atom, learns to respond to the vibrations of the mineral kingdom, and by and by, when conditions are ripe, it goes on to the kingdom of life, where, through its per-

manent physical atom, it learns through many experiences how to manifest in form.

Here we must glance at the theory of group-souls. As you know, science does not tell us anything of the psychic or subjective side of evolution, yet such a side must exist. We are unable to interpret life in terms of mechanism ; we can only do so in terms of life and mind. The evolution so much talked of presupposes a preceding involution, for you cannot unfold what is not already within.

The rough sketch given is a mere hint at the process of involution, after which we began our preparation for the mighty ascent. Thus when life is withdrawn from the physical form, we know it does not cease to be, but we do not know where it goes ; for if life if immortal it must be somewhere. We have to postulate—though with some it is a certainty—a psychic plane contiguous to the world of life, where the experiences gained in form can be assimilated and expanded, so that further effort may be made.

This psychic plane is the world of fairy, and these delicate beings are said to play an important part in the mediation of the life-forces from the inner planes to the outer. As experience is gained, it is assimilated, and further effort can be made and new forms appear, until at last we reach the human standard. Originally the many forms of life are in groups, and each member of any group contributes something of its development to the whole. There is no individual life ; that is, no consciousness of individuality in the many forms belonging to any group, though there is a growing towards it. As we ascend the ladder of evolution, so we find the groups becoming smaller, until at last complete self-consciousness is achieved.

Up to this point, those who believe in only one human life on earth will probably agree with the re-incarnationist.

The one-lifer, if I may so term him, argues that when life reaches individuality there is no further need for it to return to this plane ; that as the path of progress is open, we can go on and continue our growth on the higher planes of being. It sounds reasonable, but the re-incarnationist argues that the doctrine of emergence is not morally satisfying, in that we see men are in various stages of growth, and the inequalities of life on this plane are not accounted for.

Those who espouse the theory of emergence argue that as we are parts of one whole, the experiences of individuals contribute to it, and that as we advance we shall be enabled to share all the experiences of life. He argues that our advance is from an amorphous consciousness to individuality, and from this to an expansion to total consciousness.

In reply, the re-incarnationist argues that it is not reasonable to suppose that one can become master of the physical plane during one incarnation.

In reply to this the emergist says that as we have come up through the various kingdoms from mineral to man, there are in our larger consciousness all the experiences gained during our evolution, and that as we go on in the higher planes we shall be able to bring these to the surface of our minds and make intelligent use of them.

So we may go on, both sides speculating ; and it is the moral argument which for many turns the scale in favour of re-incarnation. We must examine this.

Every spiritualist preaches very emphatically the

doctrine of personal responsibility ; but if the emergist is right there seems to be a grave injustice. It does not satisfy one whose life has been one of constant struggle and frustration, who has made frequent sacrifices for principle and had to suffer in consequence, to be told that he is contributing valuable experiences to the whole. What he feels is a sense of injustice ; for if the body he receives is, through hereditary bias, predisposed to a certain type of life, where does his choice come in ? On the other hand, the re-incarnationist argues that personal responsibility is inherent, and we only reap what we sow. Thus the kind of body we receive *is predetermined by ourselves through the kind of life or lives we have lived on earth before.* He says that just as form in any kingdom registers the standard of development reached by the informing life, so does the body we receive on incarnating indicate the standard of development reached by the ego making use of it. It must be made clear that there is no re-incarnation of personalities ; there is only re-incarnation of the real self for purposes of fuller growth and development.

The personality is merely a mask, it hides as much as it reveals, and none of us has seen one another—we only perceive one another's forms or personalities. The real self is for ever hidden. If the long process of evolution has been necessary to bring out the latent qualities of the ego so that it may acquire a *consciousness* of immortality, are we to infer that one manifestation in human form is enough ? May not the ego manifest periodically when it is necessary for it to do so ? Let us proceed further. When death comes, we pass into the next plane of life, where we still gather experiences and go from plane to plane, until we reach the ego's home. There all the experiences gathered by the personality are absorbed in the ego, personality persisting in the real self as memory. That is, personal consciousness expands to that of the ego, becoming one with it, and sharing in all the experiences of preceding personalities and all those gained in our pre-human life in the group-soul.

When it is necessary for its further growth, the ego manifests afresh, and sets in operation those forces which previous incarnations have generated; another root is put out into material existence and a new personality comes into being, governed by the law which guides the manifestation of the ego to that country and to those parents with whom it is in karmic relationship. The new body expresses in some degree the sum-total of development reached in previous lives, plus the extra power for further advance.

It will be seen that the question of memory of past lives can only be realized as increased power. Faculty is memory, it has been said, but the main point to bear in mind is, that whatever theory we favour, the consciousness of immortality is something *won by effort*, and it may be lost by persistent evil. Personal responsibility is far more real than many spiritualists imagine. It is fondly said that all will be saved, that at last God will bring all His children home. We hope so; but suppose the child refuses to go home?

One of the principles subscribed to by all who become members of the "Spiritualists' National Union" is "a path of progress open to every soul that *wills* to tread it". The important word is "wills". What of those who will *not* tread it? If personal responsibility is a fact, as we are assured it is, there can be no coercion. God will not force salvation upon any soul. It is offered; the means are at hand; but if any soul refuses to use them, then the results must be met. Remember the man who had only one talent and refused to use it: it was taken from him. That is the law. If you have power and do not exercise it, the means to do so perish.

Ponder on the phenomenon of parasitism. It has its corollaries in the moral world, and we ought to face these matters and not think of the Love of God as so anaemic that it overlooks positive evil. I leave the question; but it is one we should ponder. We should strive to realize the implications of our doctrine of personal responsibility.

CHAPTER V

CONCLUSION

Man a Spiritual Being—The Spiritualist Movement—The Earth a Spiritual World—Our Inner World—Last Words.

The value of any science, philosophy, or religion lies in its applicability to the problems which from time to time come before us. What we have to guard against is that we do not become hidebound. We should keep our minds alert to new aspects of truth, and be ever ready to modify our ideas in accordance with new knowledge. This study of mediumship has shown that it has a very definite bearing upon many problems of life, and the alert medium will ever strive to put into practice the results of his study. A few words will show some of the practical aspects arising from our investigations.

Man a Spiritual Being

The outstanding truth which our study has revealed is that man is a spirit now; that we are sparks of the Divine Flame, and as such must, if we desire to preserve our individuality, live according to this central fact. It is more than a matter of intellectual curiosity, or of spinning webs of metaphysical argument. The reality of life is not its manifestation in form, but its inherent power to manifest thus.

If we are spirits, then this truth demands that we endeavour to live in accordance with it. The spirit of man ever strives for harmony—that is, health—and this means all-round aliveness; a condition in which body, soul, and spirit, are in such agreement that the ego is master of the forces of life and can direct them to given ends. The universe is intelligent in every part. We have seen how that intelligence is ever manifest, so that we have law and order. But it is not enough that the universe be intelligent, it must also be good. In our considerations we have noted that good is the power which builds, evil that which destroys: good is considerate of others, evil of self alone. The former makes for more abundant life, the latter for restriction, frustration, and death. It will be seen that if we realize the truth of our spiritual nature, we shall view life from within, instead of being swept along its surface amidst a whirl of contending loyalties.

Another truth emerges. Our spiritual life is only isolated in its individuality, not in its wholeness. The consciousness of self-hood springs from a deeper self, the Infinite Self. Consciousness of this truth introduces us to the religion of the Spirit. We see underneath the faiths of men there is one co-ordinating power, which is righteous and good, which moves the hearts of men so that they experience an urge for self-expression and worship. Religion is a flower native to the soul, which springs from the heath of our spiritual being, and its fragrance and beauty are in accordance with the growth of our spiritual nature.

Now the fact that we are "Sons of God", as St. John says, is full of power, for it indicates that we may become God-like. This truth has been seized upon by some minds and degraded to merely personal ends. If we wish to see what it means to be God-like, we must go to our New Testament and read the life of Him who, for us, has revealed in fullest manner the nature of God. There we find expressed that abandonment to the ideals of the spirit in which everything is renounced until only one principle remains, the principle of service.

We must seek, not for the sake of self-development, or to wield great and marvellous powers, but that we may be worthy servitors at the altar of life. Though our consciousness of self has been so hardly won, and is usually so intensely held, we must not live in self. We have to learn to forget self, to put it on one side, give it up, lose it, seeking only that one may minister to the whole. "He that loseth his life shall find it." It is the law, and we must come to this if we are to reach the higher levels of the spiritual life.

Now take this principle of service, unite it to the concept of our being spirits now, and gaze over the world, asking why this turmoil, unrest, and suffering. And you will see it arises from an infringement of this fundamental law. *Selfishness is blind.* Some talk of enlightened selfishness ; that is merely a modification and restraint of the grosser views of selfishness, in order to increase the essential power of the self by maintaining what is actually an unjust state of affairs. The abandonment of self does not mean its destruction, but its liberation. If we could but collectively apply the principle of service to our social life we should find most of our problems would cease. All the problems of our social life are self-created. They are the result of an individualism run riot, of a competition which destroys. Obedience to the jungle law, "the struggle for life and the survival of the fittest", in our social life can only result in lowering of ethical standards, and giving an opportunity to the most ruthless to climb over the bodies of their fellows to success. We are now reaping the results of this gross materialism in the perplexity and suffering which afflict us.

I am not here concerned with political theories, only with the individual application of a truth. For the salvation of the world must begin by men experiencing a change of both heart and head. Religion is first an individual matter, but once we realize its power and how we are linked with the source of Divine Being, we must become channels through which the fertilizing love of the Spirit may manifest. We begin to build for eternity. Time ceases to have any importance for us. We gaze beyond the confines of earth and see life continuing its evolution to ever increasing heights of grandeur. Such vision should hearten us, should give us the strength needed to live amidst the contending interests of this lower state. And if the vision demands of us sacrifice, the laying down of our lives in suffering, let us think of Him who went bravely to the cross, and pray for the courage to emulate His example.

The Spiritualist Movement

When we look over the field of spiritualistic activities, we cannot help but see how little the intrinsic powers of the spirit are realized, even amongst piritualists and mediums. Indeed, at the present time there is a very decided form of materialistic spiritism in evidence. The exploitation of psychic power by certain people is a denial of the truths for which we stand. Difficult circumstances are often pleaded as an excuse for the lowering of tone so often observed. It is not sufficiently realized that even here some effort might be made to raise the standard of spiritual life; but there is an indifference to spiritual values, due, in some measure, to the manner in which the doctrine of progression is taught.

There is no grasp of the law, and one sometimes hears spiritualists say: "It's all right, I can make it up on the other side." Any notion more soul-deadening and destructive of spiritual values can hardly be conceived. Also, the tendency to throw over what the past has given us, a tendency springing from a false vanity, has led to a narrowing of ideas resulting in the introduction of sectarian influences, all of which reveal how difficult it is to keep a truth free from the entangling influences of organization. Organizations often start with the idea of liberating souls, but in many cases end by imprisoning them. We all have lessons to learn, and perhaps spiritualists in the mass have to win their way to that freedom which they imagine they now enjoy. Illusions can be very comforting, but let us be sure about the facts and not rest in a false security. Here again we see the need of applying the principle of service, and realizing that we are spirits now.

One of the dangers of our movement today is, that by its concentration of attention upon phenomena, it is encouraging a false dependence upon the unseen. When we consider the number of people who grow into the habit of consulting mediums about the ordinary and trivial affairs of daily life, we see how spirit-intercourse of this kind can be a source of weakness. We should seek to develop our own resources. No one is without some degree of intuition, no one is without the power to pray and ask for guidance, and no one who trusts will ever be without it.

One can understand the protest of the prophet against consulting wizards and those who have a familiar spirit. God knows we see enough of it in these days, and much that passes for psychic work is no more than common fortune-telling. If we know that we are spirits, we shall realize that within us lie those potentialities and powers which alone can help us. The best our friends in the unseen can do for us is to offer advice and guidance, but they cannot live our lives, they can only live their own. Hence, when one views the field of spiritualistic activities and sees how little the meaning of Spiritualism is realized by those who claim to be spiritualists, it is not a very encouraging spectacle. No wonder so many pass through the ranks of Spiritualism and leave in disgust at its materialism.

Outside Spiritualism, one feels more hopeful. Fortunately, what is known as Spiritualism is not confined to its organized expression. Those in spirit-life who have the welfare of the movement under their care and guidance do not confine their activities to one channel. Wherever there is an opening or an opportunity, they are active, and probably it is through science rather than through the narrow sectarianism of organized Spiritualism that the world will receive most benefit. If the leaders do not awake to their responsibilities and strive to mould a more intelligent opinion amongst the rank and file, the leadership will pass out of their hands, and the dream of one prominent spiritualist, that the churches will absorb Spiritualism, will be nearer realization.

After all, those who guide from the unseen are above our petty weaknesses and desires to organize a great movement. They wish it to be a permeating force, helpful to all religions. It is said there are no sects in heaven, and, rightly understood, there should be none in Spiritualism. It belongs to no one section of men, but to humanity. To seek to limit it, as some do, is to betray those in the higher life, and once again to bind upon the minds of men the shackles of creedalism. Even among spiritualists the spirit of the old inquisitors yet lives. The price of freedom is eternal vigilance.

The Earth a Spiritual World

Another thought emerges from the truth that we are spirits now: it is that this world is as much a spiritual world as any other realm of existence. Matter, time, and space are the tools which God uses to express His creative powers. In itself matter is neither evil nor good; it is a means whereby God tells us something about Himself. It is natural that we should long for something beyond what earth can give us; but think for a moment what life on earth would be if we reached that degree of spiritual awareness and understanding in which all our problems were solved, and we had learned to be as the angels of heaven! What a transformation would come over the world! We should have peace, goodwill, harmony, joy, and all the grace and sweetness of heaven here on earth.

I can conceive of life on earth being as heavenly as life in the higher realms.

I believe that one day it will be so, and mediumship rightly understood should help us to look upon the world as one of the workshops of God, where He is fashioning the Divine Image in which it is said He created man. Surely this should give us renewed strength to strive towards establishing the Kingdom of Heaven here.

The old concept of matter as something evil is false. It is our duty to prove it false: so to live that the world can afford us the opportunity of expressing our inner life in loveliness and grace. Even now, when we get close to the heart of Nature and are able to see her beauty, we feel how near is the Spirit of God. If we are perplexed, and we are about many things; if we suffer, and we often do in many ways; if we have lost our peace of mind and are distressed—let us turn to Nature, who never betrays those who trust her; and in the quietness of the countryside, or even in our own small gardens, seek that peace and solace which our common Mother can give. Through her heart the Father speaks, and in the sough of the wind through the trees may be heard the whispers of angels, and in the beauty of the wayside flowers the reflected glory of a fairer world.

Our Inner World

I have suggested that spiritual communion gives us a far richer experience of the higher life than mere conversations with our arisen friends can convey. We live in many worlds, and each of us has a life of his own hidden from his fellows. This hidden life is, perhaps, the most important; it is a world where we know ourselves as *we really are.* It is possible that we may, for a time, deceive ourselves, but in those moments of quiet introspection we see ourselves, not alone as others see us—for they can only draw inferences from what they observe—but as we really are.

One of the truths which religion has preserved, and upon which our friends in the higher life have thrown some light, is the truth of judgment. As we progress in life it is wise to have periods of spiritual stock-taking, of striving to know ourselves in all honesty. To take off the blinkers of self-deceit, and review our strivings and endeavours. By such means—and it should be done in a *healthy* and *not* a morbid spirit—we shall discover where we are weak, whether we have grown, and if the set of the spirit is true to its ideals.

The importance of this is that our outer life tends, more and more, to reflect our inner world. What we hold strongly in thought tends to work itself out on the material plane. Man tends to become what he thinks. That is, character reveals the kind of inner world we inhabit. In the life of the spirit there come times when it is necessary to have cleansings. We are informed by our friends that when we enter spirit-life we shall have to face the results of our life here, assess its value, review our existence, and see what we have made of life generally. This, they say, is what is meant by judgment. There is no need to leave this until we pass over. Much of it can be done now, but do not turn inward and grieve over lost opportunities and deplore your lack of strength. For purposes of growth this must be done in a rational spirit. Morbidness must be avoided, and any review of our life must be undertaken, not from motives of self-pity, but from a keen desire to increase power and capacity to serve. The world of man within is as varied and as beautiful as the world without. Bring them into harmony, and many of the difficulties of life will fade out in a greater understanding.

Last Words

If I seem to have stressed the personal point of view in this chapter, it is merely that we may understand that it is not a matter of merely academic interest, but of individual development. These questions go to the roots of religion, and we can see that Spiritualism does not seek to supplant Christianity, as some seem to fear, but to supplement it. If it differs from creedal Christianity, it is at one with the essential principles enunciated by Jesus. Every one of the principles laid down by the two great sections of the Spiritualist Movement in this country are drawn as much from Christian as from what are called purely spiritualistic sources. The purpose of those in spirit-life has been, and is, to emphasize certain principles, and by scientific demonstration to drive into our consciousness the truths of religion. They are not animated by any bias other than that of seeking to give us the clearest light upon life we are able to bear. As we are each in different stages of development, so do we each see in accordance therewith. This variety should make for a keener enjoyment, a more virile mental life, and an enrichment of our spiritual being.

If this book has opened doors in your minds, shed light in any darkened corner of your world, encouraged you to persevere in the endeavour to climb the heights of spiritual attainment, it has done all that I have wished. In taking leave of you, I do so with the hope that the light given has been clear and undimmed by partisanship or self-seeking. We are seekers, and those who seek have the promise that they shall find. And what we find we must share with others, so that together we may reach the Kingdom of God.

THE END

www.ingramcontent.com/pod-product-compliance
Ingram Content Group UK Ltd.
Pitfield, Milton Keynes, MK11 3LW, UK
UKHW020415250726
13967UKWH00007B/2648

9 781948 986564